# Out of the Darkness

## TEENS AND SUICIDE

Marion Crook

ARSENAL
PULP PRESS
*Vancouver*

OUT OF THE DARKNESS
Copyright © 2003 by Marion Crook

ARSENAL PULP PRESS
103-1014 Homer Street
Vancouver, B.C.
Canada  V6B 2W9
*arsenalpulp.com*

The publisher gratefully acknowledges the support of the Canada Council for the Arts and the British Columbia Arts Council for its publishing program, and the Government of Canada through the Book Publishing Industry Development Program for its publishing activities.

Book and cover design by Solo
Cover photograph by Thomas Hoeffgen/Getty Images
Printed and bound in Canada

NATIONAL LIBRARY OF CANADA
CATALOGUING IN PUBLICATION DATA:
Crook, Marion, 1941–
Out of the darkness : teens talk about suicide / Marion Crook.

ISBN 1-55152-141-5

1. Teenagers – Suicidal behavior. 2. Suicide – Psychological aspects. 3. Suicide – Prevention. 4. Teenagers – Interviews. I. Title.
HV6546.C758 2003    362.28'0835    C2003-910380-3

# Contents

# Acknowledgments

I would like the thank all the teens who responded to my ads in the newspapers and called or met with me. They were genuine, compassionate, and committed to helping other teens. The Canadian Mental Health Association (BC Division) and the Suicide Information and Education Centre in Calgary, the Distress Centre in Toronto, and the Helpline in Halifax offered practical help and encouragement. Carol Lowe, Program Director of the Vancouver Crisis Centre, gave me much needed advice and information over the many months it took to prepare the manuscript. I would like to thank Peter Gajdis, Julie Epp, and Angela Haggerty who reviewed my questions and the chapter on suicide risk and offered invaluable advice. Jasha Ramsay, Executive Director of the Vancouver Crisis Centre, gave me initial encouragement and continual support. Thanks also to Chloe Lapp of the Canadian Mental Health Association and Gordon Winch and Ila Rutlege of the Toronto Distress Centre. Many thanks to Rhamona Von Browning of Youth Quest; Neena Tragguason of the Vancouver Women's Health Collective; Geri from the Lesbian Support Group; Heather Stenerson, Friends for Life, Saskatchewan; Sherryl Mydonick, Yorkton, Saskatchewan; Darien Simons, Vancouver Crisis Centre, who studied the book and recommended improvements; Corporal Wayne Price, Aboriginal Policing, RCMP; Rodney Louie, Lilooet Tribal Council, who offered comments and direction; and Matthew and Ashley Lindsay of Winnipeg, who gave me room and board and introduced me to their friends.

I also wish to acknowledge the Vancouver Crisis Centre; the United Church of Canada, Van Dusen Fund; and the Chris Spencer Foundation for their assistance in providing grants and encouragement for research.

The poems in this book were donated by some of the teens I interviewed. I received too many to include them all, and I wish to thank everyone who was willing to participate with their ideas, emotions, and commitment to helping others.

*to Bobbie*
*and the many teens*
*who contributed to this book*

# Preface

*Round the corner*
*Hide from the darkness*
*that follows my footsteps*
*that lives on my fears*

– Megan

Teenagers try suicide. I know they can have a difficult time – I worked as a public health nurse for a number of years and had been a resource for troubled teens, but I had never saw suicide as a problem I could do anything about. When I first became interested in researching the problem I had teenagers of my own at home and discovered that suicide was an alarming and increasing choice for many young people. I had thought myself an alert parent, teaching safe sex and safe driving habits, concerned about hitchhiking, drug and alcohol use, and the necessity of a good academic life, but I never thought about talking to my children about suicide. My understanding of teens and suicide was based on the lectures in my nursing education and the limiting and erroneous belief that suicide was usually a result of mental illness. I could see that the teens who died by suicide were not mentally ill, nor did they look much different from other teens. Still, I did nothing about my observations.

I wrote a book about how teenagers feel about being adopted (*The Face in the Mirror: Teenagers and Adoption*, Arsenal Pulp Press), based on research with forty teens. When the book hit the stores I received a telephone call from a woman who had read it, who knew I could write, and who wanted me to take her daughter Bobbie's diary and make a book from it.

"You're an author," she said. "Do something!"

Her daughter had kept a diary and a journal, snippets of ideas and some poems, from the time she was sixteen until the age of twenty-one, when she killed herself. The girl's brother had also comitted suicide. Their mother thought that if I could study Bobbie's written work, I might find out why and be able to help others. I said, "No, I can't do it. I'm not a psychiatrist. I don't know enough." Bobbie's mother sent me her daughter's writing anyway. She was determined. But I was similarly determined to avoid them. They remained unread on the floor of my study for months. When I moved from central British Columbia to the west coast, I took the writings with me. I had too much conscience to throw them away, but not enough to read them. They seemed to scream at me from their position on the floor, demanding attention while I tried my best to ignore them.

I finally caved in and read all Bobbie's writings. It was a very sad and moving experience, but even after that, I knew I couldn't write about Bobbie. I felt that telling only her story would not help readers much; it was simply too sad. Perhaps, I thought, other teenagers who had tried suicide and not completed it could tell me what made it seem like such a good idea, and, perhaps, those teenagers could pass on advice on what persuaded them not to try suicide again. I could write a positive book.

I still did not want to write it. It seemed such a huge undertaking. I approached the Vancouver Crisis Centre for advice. Wouldn't such a book encourage teens to try suicide? No, they told me, no one wants to talk about suicide; everyone wants to pretend that it doesn't happen, or that it happens by accident. Teens need more information. They need to know what to look for, what to beware of, and where to go. Do the work. Write the book. We're behind you.

I then went to the Canadian Mental Health Association. The executive director there told me she really wanted me to do the research and write the book, and that she and her office staff would do all they could to help me. It seemed as though there was a tremendous need; that teenagers needed a book that told them what other teens felt, what they wanted, how they coped. I'd tentatively put my foot in the water and a strong current was pulling me under.

With the assistance of the Chris Spencer Foundation, the United Church of Canada, Van Dusen Fund, the Canadian Mental Health Association (BC Division), a group of three young people in Vancouver (my advisory board), and the Distress Centre in Toronto, I started interviewing.

At first, I was afraid that the questionnaire I composed would not be good enough, that I would have to phone everyone I interviewed, months later, to ask vital questions I hadn't thought of until the research was finished. At this time I did not yet have my PhD and was a beginning researcher with many concerns about my ability. But a medical researcher who listened to my plans told me to go ahead: I was on the right track. At this point I needed a lot of encouragement.

With the expectations of so many people pressuring me, I couldn't put off the project any longer. I had to get out there and ask the questions that I needed answers to.

So I spent one summer in fast food restaurants and other locations across Canada interviewing teens who had attempted suicide. I advertised in the newspapers, looking for teens willing to talk about their experience, and they called in, willing to talk to me, willing to tell me what other teens should know. I met them at McDonald's on Yonge Street in Toronto and in downtown Winnipeg, at the Burger King, Swenson's, on park benches, in their homes. I sat in the sun on Granville Island in Vancouver and talked to a teen for two hours. I got lost in Calgary driving around a cemetery three times before locating a teen's house. I sat on a bench in Trinity Square in Toronto growing colder by the minute while a teen told me what it was like to be so alone that death seemed better than any life she could imagine. There were so many who responded, I couldn't meet all who called me. I couldn't listen to that much emotion without absorbing some of it, and had to go off by myself for at least an hour between interviews. I needed a little time to bring my own emotions into equilibrium. It was a long summer.

Some teens I spoke to still lived with their parents. Sometimes their parents didn't know that they had tried suicide and the teens didn't want me to tell them, which I respected. Sometimes we talked in their homes while the parents stayed in the back yard or the kitchen, never coming in to ask me why I was there. I was amazed that they were so understanding. Sometimes the teens knew their parents would never understand and, without telling them, met me elsewhere. I met teens after work on their way home, in the Eaton Centre in Toronto, at the Conservatory in Vancouver, on the only hill I saw in Calgary, on the dock in Halifax.

An interview usually lasted an hour and a half. The shortest was forty minutes, because I had to leave to catch a plane, the longest was two hours and forty-five minutes. I felt privileged with each one.

Because I didn't want my ideas to be shaped by adults, I tried not to read much of the professional literature before I talked to the teens. After talking to some of them, I started to hear recurring themes: how they felt life hemmed them in, oppressed them, how they felt they had few choices. Each one told me a different story, but often spoke of similar problems.

After I had completed the interviews with teens, I read the literature on teen suicide written by psychiatrists, psychologists, sociologists, parents, and counsellors, and talked to professionals. I also spoke to parents of teens, television and radio show hosts, and callers on talk shows in Oklahoma, Colorado, California, New York, Halifax, Vancouver, and many, many places between. I became more involved in the community, helping to organize a conference on suicide prevention, intervention, and postvention, and sat on a committee that guided the creation of a provincial suicide prevention plan for high schools. I also worked with the many dedicated and knowledgeable teens and adults who try hard to help teens avoid suicide.

Over the past few years I have noted the increasing number of suicide prevention programs available for teens, as well as the increasing concerns of parents, school staff, and professionals. The media regularly report stories of murder and suicide in schools, bullying, drug overdoses, alcohol abuse, and the many difficult choices that teens face on a daily basis. Awareness of teen suicide is growing. I am hopeful that this means teens will get more help when they feel they have nowhere to go.

The teens I interviewed inspired me. I admired their courage, their independence, and their ability to finally believe in themselves. So many are truly fine people, courageous and generous. They added their voices, their expectations, to those of the personnel of the Crisis Centre and the Mental Health Association and the Foundations who supported me. Everyone wanted me to write what would be useful and important. At times I felt the pressure of wanting to do them justice. On one particularly difficult evening I imagined all those voices calling to me from the walls of my office. I dove into the arms of my nearest and dearest and wailed about my lack of ability. Then I started to write.

This book talks about the teens I met, their problems, how they coped with them, and what they thought parents, professionals, and other teens should do if faced with similar challenges. It looks at teen suicide from the point of view of those who have gone through the crisis of adolescence.

This book is not a dramatization of the horrors of teen life; it is simply the reality of that life. Readers should not be discouraged by these stories. They should understand better what teens feel when they contemplate suicide – and thus be better able to help them.

# ONE

## *The Way It Is*

*The acts of defiance*
*There is no reliance*
*to what was then and*
*what is now.*
*Overcast greys biding down*
*They take the rejected*
*The street, the neglected*
*In the desolate night ghostly lies*
*Tears within trees of suspicious eyes*
*All the emotions, the dark sides*
*of life fought*
*Time deceives devotions, singles out our*
*wicked thoughts*
*Transformation, Termination, Situation, Animation*
*The games that are played to fuck up*
*our minds*
*The fearless monsters we think are our kind*
*The changes we take, the evil we love*
*The insane things we have all done*
*No one has won.*

*Mindgames.*

– Diana

When I was a child no one in my class or even my school died by suicide. No one even talked about it. Today, suicide is the third cause of death of young people in the USA, behind accidents and homicides.[1] In Canada, suicide is the second cause of death for teens, with accidents being the first.[2] The very concept of suicide as an ongoing, constant problem among teens seems amazing. How did this happen? It can't be explained as if it were an infection that swept over the continent on a wave of invading bacteria. Suicide is a physical act, committed intentionally under the guise of individual choice, taking place in a society that offers that choice; a society that culturally and socially influences teens to view suicide as a viable option.

## THE STATISTICS

Statistics can offer us a glimpse of the realities of teen suicide. In most countries where information is available, in the fifteen to twenty-four-year-old age group (there are no separate statistics for the teen years of thirteen to nineteen), more young men complete the act of suicide while more young women attempt it. In most countries the ratio of suicide by young males to females ranges from eleven males to one female (in Ireland) to ten males to six females (in Sweden).[3] The suicide rate rose from the 1950s to the 1980s and today remains a steady, entrenched threat to the lives of teens.

The suicide rates provide us with only a partial understanding of the problem. The rates themselves are not necessarily accurate – they are probably low. Many countries report some suicides as "accidents" which do not appear in the statistics. Some communities view suicide as a religious and moral transgression, so out of compassion for the surviving family, officials are reluctant to label the death as suicide, again calling it an "accident." Some insurance companies do not pay out to the family of a suicide; this also can influence the person signing the death certificate. Although the World Health Organization devised a system of designating a death as suicide in 1900, many countries do not follow it, or have different criteria. In some countries, a death is declared a suicide on the basis of a "balance of probabilities" – the most likely reason for the deaths – and on the concept of "beyond a reasonable doubt," where suicide must be proven. This creates big differences in reporting. Because countries have different criteria for determining suicide and different forms upon which to record it, they extract different information, resulting in uneven and unequal statistics. Bearing in mind the problems with recording suicide as a statistic and the fact that suicides are notoriously under-reported throughout the world, statistics indicate at least some degree of the problem without telling us everything we need to know.

Statistics usually tell us the number of young people who die by suicide, their gender, and in some countries, details of their lives (see Table 1).

## Table 1

### SUICIDES IN COUNTRIES AROUND THE WORLD
*ages 15–24, 1991–1993, rates per 100,000*

| Country | M | F | Ratio |
|---|---|---|---|
| Greece | 3.8 | 0.8 | 5 |
| Portugal | 4.3 | 2.0 | 2 |
| Italy | 5.7 | 1.6 | 4 |
| Spain | 7.1 | 2.2 | 3 |
| Netherlands | 9.1 | 3.8 | 2 |
| Sweden | 10.0 | 6.7 | 1 |
| Japan | 10.0 | 4.4 | 2 |
| Israel | 11.7 | 2.5 | 5 |
| UK | 12.2 | 2.3 | 5 |
| Germany | 12.7 | 3.4 | 4 |
| Denmark | 13.4 | 2.3 | 6 |
| France | 14.0 | 4.3 | 3 |
| Bulgaria | 15.4 | 5.6 | 3 |
| Czech Rep. | 16.4 | 4.3 | 4 |
| Poland | 16.6 | 2.5 | 7 |
| Ukraine | 17.2 | 5.3 | 3 |
| Hungary | 19.1 | 5.5 | 3 |
| Austria | 21.1 | 6.5 | 3 |
| Ireland | 21.5 | 2.0 | 11 |
| USA | 21.9 | 3.8 | 6 |
| Belarus | 24.2 | 5.2 | 5 |
| Canada | 24.7 | 6.0 | 4 |
| Switzerland | 25.0 | 4.8 | 5 |
| Australia | 27.3 | 5.6 | 5 |
| Norway | 28.2 | 5.2 | 5 |
| Estonia | 29.7 | 10.6 | 3 |
| Finland | 33.0 | 3.2 | 10 |
| Latvia | 35.0 | 9.3 | 4 |
| Slovenia | 37.0 | 8.4 | 4 |
| New Zealand | 39.9 | 6.2 | 6 |
| Russian Fed. | 41.7 | 7.9 | 5 |
| Lithuania | 44.9 | 6.7 | 7 |

*World Suicide Facts 1993*[4]

Information from China, not included in the statistics in Table 1, reveals a different trend among young people. In China, according to figures recorded between 1995 and 1999 by researchers headed by Dr Michael Phillips at the Beijing Hui Long Guan Hospital, nineteen percent of the deaths among people fifteen to thirty-four are suicides. The rates for young women are twenty-five percent higher than those for men. They are even worse in rural areas where one-third of all deaths in women aged twenty-five to thirty-four were suicides. It is the leading cause of death for women and the second cause for men. This is quite a different picture from the rest of the world – and researchers believe these statistics to be conservative.[5] What is happening in China that women are more likely to kill themselves than they are in, say, Italy? Do the Italian statistics hide suicide, while the Chinese statistics report it? Should we be looking for social, cultural, psychological, or even religious reasons as influencing young people?

Large differences in the rates of suicide between countries and within countries stimulate speculation about how the country and culture influences teens' decision to die by suicide. What social, physical, psychological, and cultural factors influence a teen to try suicide? There is some research that sheds light on this.

We know that gender seems to play a part. In the United States the comparison between boys and girls shows that, until boys and girls are nine years old, their suicide rates are the same; from ten to fourteen, the boys' rate is twice the girls'; from fifteen to nineteen, four times; and from twenty to twenty-four, six times.[6] Boys tend to use more lethal means and, therefore, complete the act more often (except in China). Girls tend to attempt more often, but with less lethal means, although this may be changing as girls gain more access to firearms.

These statistics indicate that suicide is part of youth society. Scholars have taken these statistics and tried to relate them to aspects of teens' lives in order to look for causes of suicide, ways to strengthen resiliency, and ways to create a social environment in which suicide is less likely. Like much research, these numerous studies give researchers specific clues about the larger picture of teen suicide. There is still a great deal of speculation about what the statistics mean and whether they are reliable enough to use.

There are, within the statistics for a particular country, clusters that get lost in the general reporting. In the UK, for instance, the rate for young men was 12.2 in 1997. Included in that statistic was the rate for young men in Scotland, which was thirty-three per 100,000 – a high rate which was hidden in the over-all UK report. New Zealand's rate for 1999 in this age group is males 30.6 and females 14.2; the male rate has come down from the high level of the past, but the female rate has gone up. Another look at New Zealand statistics for 1999 shows the rate for non-Maori males is 27.7, the Maori males 42.4.[7] There is speculation around these numbers, but there is room for bias, and a temptation to simplify very complex situations.

In Canada, aboriginal teens die by suicide five to six times more often than non-Native teens.[8] They share similar feelings of hopelessness and powerlessness with non-Native teens, but also have a unique perspective. Studies on the relationship of aboriginal culture to suicide show the way in which colonization contributes to increased suicide (Royal Commission on Aboriginal Peoples, 1995). People who have been taught that they are inferior and do not deserve a future can internalize that belief until they act as if it were so. Without the hope of a positive future, suicide is more likely. As well, many aboriginal people, as part of the process of colonization, suffer from poverty, geographical isolation, and low employment opportunities. Housing is also a problem on some reserves. It is difficult for young people to move away from home because there are few places for them to go. These contribute to feelings of hopelessness and powerlessness which can lead to suicide.

Gay and lesbian teens can see similar bleakness in their futures. They experience prejudice, harassment, humiliation, and rejection from society and their families. It is this societal rejection that contributes to their suicide ideation. Studies show a higher rate of suicide among gay and lesbian teens; a Massachusetts study reported thirty percent of gay and lesbian teens died by suicide.[9] Even if that study is wrong and the rate is lower, it is still too high. Social prejudice, harassment, and even persecution will affect a teen's perspective on life and death.

Statistics give us the numbers we need to establish the problem, and can be useful to grab the attention of those who have no idea that suicide is so insidious. The numbers are less useful in trying to determine why teens choose suicide and what teens, parents, and helping professionals can do about it. We need to go further than the statistics take us.

Because suicide is the second or third cause of death among young people, it seems highly likely that most teens have at least thought about it. Most of the teens I interviewed had never told anyone about their suicide attempts, so they, and teens like them, are not included in the statistics. No doubt there are thousands of teens whose suicide attempts are not reflected in statistics. It seems best to assume that since many teens try suicide, many deaths are unreported as suicide, and suicide attempts are very often unreported, teens thinking about suicide must be more common than we think. We can't prove this statistically, but it seems a reasonable assumption.

## SEARCHING FOR REASONS IN SOCIETY

What makes so many teens choose suicide? I thought that by asking those who had attempted it, I could find this out. I did discover why individuals thought suicide was a reasonable option, and this book tells the stories of those who tried, but in my interviews with them I did not discover why, approximately thirty to forty years ago, suicide rates rose all over the world and remain unbearably high today.

The teens I spoke to, making painful choices about their lives and their particular circumstances, did not see themselves as representative of teens around the world. They saw themselves in their own social world, but not necessarily part of a larger culture. We must look to professionals and those who work with teens and study the phenomenon of suicide to understand what might be the underlying social cause.

"We never even thought of it when I was a kid," the late Peter Gzowski, renowned Canadian broadcaster, said to one of the teens from my interview group who had offered to be on his radio program. "We had troubles, but we didn't think we could solve them with suicide."

"Peter," the young teen said, exasperation in her voice, "you aren't listening."

While Peter spoke in general terms, concerned that contemporary teens seemed to reach for a drastic answer to problems that he and his generation had never considered, and worried about why an entire generation of teens would look for a solution to problems in death, the teen could see only her own immediate circumstances and was frustrated that the conversation was veering away from her own experience. Teens generally aren't willing to philosophize about the phenomenon of suicide when they are dealing with its immediate threat.

## HISTORY OF THOUGHT AROUND SUICIDE

### Social Integration

Emile Durkheim (1897),[10] a French sociologist, thought that suicide was related to the individual's ability to integrate socially: do you feel you belong in your social group or don't you? He was one of the first to write about the relationship of suicide to society. He believed that societies encouraged acceptance by and integration into a society, or discouraged it, and that the result was an increase or decrease in the incidence of suicide. It may be, as Durkheim believes, that individuals who feel that they do not belong in society want out of it. Although there are other explanations for why those individuals who feel isolated make this choice, Durkheim might be right, and society might be a huge influence on a teen's choice to live or die. Durkheim also believed that religious affiliation influences the suicide rate, not because the theology is influential – people don't choose life because they are believers, but because some religions are more tightly socially organized and controlling of individuals than others. This puts an interesting spin on the influence of organized religion. The more socially controlling, according to Durkheim, the less likely adherents will be to try suicide.

### Freedom

Within teen culture today is a great deal of freedom of choice, which, according to some scholars, is a problem. The freedom teens have to make their own choices, and a lack of control by adults, allows for the possibility of the choice of suicide. This is the view of Georges Minois (1999)[11] who suggests that the rise of suicidal behaviour parallels the rise of freedom in society. With the increasing power to make many choices, individuals also have the power to make the choice of whether to live or die. So, speculating on Minois' view that freedom creates a more likely environment for suicide, could it be that when teens do not have many choices, they may not see themselves as powerful enough to make the big choice of suicide? That may answer Peter Gzowski's question about why teens in his generation didn't consider suicide as an option: they had fewer choices in their teenaged years.

With the greater freedom to make choices in today's society, and the responsibility to make those choices, do teens feel life is too difficult, too painful, and, perhaps, too overwhelming in its dizzying array of choices? Would they be happier with less freedom? The choices themselves may be much more important than they were decades ago, although the choice to go to war and die for one's country seems to have been every generation's dilemma, and was certainly important. Still, in the past, middle-class teens did not have to resist gangs in school, were not subject to as much bullying or drugs, and did not experience the fierce competition for educational space in post-secondary programs that students face today. They were not as mobile — most did not own cars or have the ability to move from place to place as they do today, nor did they have the communication tools or the present-day access to information and activities. They have many more important choices today than they had even twenty years ago, and, perhaps, it is this plethora of choices that allows them to view suicide as simply another one. Still, every generation sees itself as more complex and more oppressed than the generation before, and it may be difficult to measure the stress on an individual, but it does seem as if the current generation of young people has more freedom to make choices, and more choices to make, than previous generations. This may affect their choice of suicide.

## Leisure Time

Do teens have more time to think about themselves in today's culture? A study in Australia (Patters and Pegg, 1999)[12] examined the link between suicide and the increasing amount of leisure time young people have, and suggested a link between boredom and high-risk health behaviours such as substance abuse and mental distress. This may depend on how the teenagers view the leisure time, and how they use it. It may be that the increasing leisure time, the increasing hours where teens have no responsibilities at home or at work, contribute to a feeling of isolation and uselessness. However, there are many teens who work hard both at school and in the community to try to create a life for themselves who are also suicidal. For every explanation of the social influences on suicide ideation, contrary examples abound.

## Poverty

When looking to society for clues as to why more teens today consider suicide, it seems reasonable to look at economic status. Wouldn't the rates be down in times of prosperity and up in times of poverty? That seems to be so, as the rates were low during the two World Wars when jobs were easy to find, and high during the Depression of the 1930s. But this is not what teens told me. They did not relate their suicide attempts to poverty, or even perceived poverty. It is possible that the rates that relate to the World Wars may have something to do with Durkheim's ideas of belonging, that during war people feel that they belong to their nation, have a purpose and are useful and, therefore, more valuable. The statistics paralleling poverty and suicide may not necessarily reflect peoples' responses to poverty, but rather their responses to social integration. "Poverty" isn't a simple idea. It may contain concepts of oppression, lack of opportunity, poor nutrition, and exposure to violence – or it may not. All those factors may influence someone toward or away from suicide.

### Suicide as a Medical Diagnosis

Some researchers believe that the increasing rate of suicide is due to the increased number of young people who are mentally ill, and that the mental health of teens is deteriorating. There are studies which discuss genetics and a family's predisposition to suicide. Suicide may be related to a genetic disposition to mental disorders such as bipolar disorder and schizophrenia. Lowered serotonin is associated with depression which is in turn associated with impulsive aggression and suicide. Certainly depression is associated with the increased risk of suicide. The United States Bureau of Health and Human Services reports between ninety-three and ninety-five percent of those who died in suicide had been diagnosed with a "psychiatric illness."[13] Statistics such as these are strong indicators that mental illness and suicide are closely related. There are studies on young people that indicate a link between mental illness and suicide. Included in the idea of "mental illness" are alcohol intoxication and other substance abuse, thus suicide is associated with a time in a teen's life when normal thinking is disrupted. The relationship of suicide to substance abuse seems clear. There is certainly more drug abuse in teen society today than there was in past years, and teens who abuse drugs are more likely to die by suicide than teens who do not. Still, teens told me that it was not that the drugs made them think of suicide; it was that having considered suicide, they were more likely to act after taking drugs. And taking drugs is in itself a risk-taking venture. But while drug abuse is a physical and medical problem for the individual, it has social and cultural components. Some cultures have more drug use than others; some countries have more drug use than others.

It would be foolish to ignore compelling studies revealing a direct relationship between suicide and mental illness and conditions such as substance abuse, anxiety disorders, some borderline personality disorders, and eating disorders. It is true that mentally ill people are more likely to try suicide than those who are not. That doesn't mean, however, that a person must be mentally ill to attempt suicide.

My resistance to the idea of mental illness as the cause of suicide stems from my experience with the teens I interviewed who, with the exception of four, were not diagnosed as mentally ill or depressed. It seems unlikely that an entire teen population in the span of two or three generations has an increased incidence of mental illness. Perhaps the diagnosis of depression is more readily made today than it was years ago when there were fewer psychiatrists and less understanding of the role of depression in the lives of teens. Perhaps we are gaining understanding of the difficulties that some people face that in the past were ignored. Perhaps the diagnosis of depression or mental illness is made to cover normal unhappiness and emotional pain. It seems that we should be wary of assuming that all teens who are suicidal are also depressed. Without arguing against the idea that suicide is closely linked to psychiatric and psychological disorders for which there seems to be a great deal of evidence, I'd like to caution that it is often very difficult for friends and families and the teens themselves to recognize a mental disorder. Teens often don't present symptoms the way adults do, and diagnosis isn't always easy or even possible. I'm also concerned that teens, parents, and friends will believe that if a teen does not have a diagnosis of mental illness, they will not attempt suicide – that is simply not true.

## Complex Influences

Edwin Schneidman (1950s)[14] was an American who was fascinated by statistics and with his research background studied the statistics around

24

suicide. His studies agree with Durkheim's that social isolation plays a large part in suicide ideation, but he adds the notion that suicide is an option for unbearable psychological pain; it is an escape. Schneidman asks us to consider that suicide is a rational alternative for many people to a life of insurmountable problems, and, therefore, understandable. It doesn't stretch the imagination to see that suicide can be perceived as a rational response to pain. Other researchers suggest that psychological strategies such as tunnel vision, either-or thinking, and lack of problem-solving abilities contribute to an individual's consideration of suicide as an answer to stress. If teens aren't used to looking for alternate ways to solve problems, they may see only one answer.

Many factors contribute to the notion that suicide is an acceptable choice among teens. The problem can be considered from medical, psychological, social, and cultural perspectives. There are even philosophical and theological influences on a teen's view of suicide. Over the centuries the philosophical influences have been many and varied.

## A Short History of Suicide in Western Culture

Not everyone in our western culture has a history that goes back to Europe. The aboriginal people of this country have their own history of suicide, and the people whose ancestors came from Asia also had a history of suicide which may influence them today. It is difficult for an English-speaking researcher to find that written history, so I am offering only one version of the history of thought around suicide with the clear understanding that there are others.

As far back as the sixth century BCE, the Greeks and Romans believed that people were possessions of the gods and, therefore, the lives of humans were to be governed and disposed of by the gods. Suicide was wrong because it interfered with the plans of the gods and was in fact presumptuous – an affront to them! The fate of the populace should be left in the hands of the gods, not snatched from their control by the individual. Later, the state replaced the gods as the authority, and suicide was then deemed wrong because humans belonged to the state and could only die by suicide with permission of the state. The state could order suicide, as it did for Socrates, making the act acceptable. Plato (fifth century BCE) also argued against suicide as a choice because he agreed that the individual belonged to the state, but thought an individual had the right to choose suicide in circumstances of incurable illness. This attitude influenced western thinking for centuries. Aristotle (fourth century BCE) also considered suicide as an act against the state, and further demanded that those who attempted suicide be punished. A Roman law responding to an increased number of suicides by young people ordered that their bodies be paraded naked through the town. This idea apparently did discourage suicide attempts.

The notion that the state held supreme power over life and death continued until the Stoics (Seneca, 60 CE) who thought only soldiers and slaves should be prohibited from taking their own lives as they were clearly property of the state, although others were not. The philosophy and morality around suicide centered on who "owned" the life of the individual.[15]

In the early Christian era and the Jewish tradition, there was little concern about suicide – the Bible hardly mentions it, and doesn't censure it. In fact, some people today see Jesus' death as a suicide, a death he could have avoided but chose to accept. In the early Christian Church the notion of suicide developed into martyrdom where devout Christians offered themselves to their religion, dying to prove their devotion to the Church. Often the families of those who died by suicide were financially and socially supported by the Church. At times, suicide was urged by the Church as a way for its followers to show political protest. The Bishop of Caesarea (260–339 CE) advised his Christian followers to embrace suicide as a form of protest against the government of the time – much as modern-day zealots do. Throughout history, suicide in certain situations was approved by philosophies such as Cynicism, Epicureanism, Stoicism, and Christianity. It was St Augustine in the fourth century CE who turned the attitude toward suicide to one of prohibition and disapproval. He viewed it as wrong for much the same reasons as the early Romans – that one's body did not belong to the individual but to God or the Church and, therefore, the individual did not have the right to dispose of it. In 533 CE at the Council of Orleans, the Catholic Church denied burial to anyone who committed suicide while being accused of a crime because the individual was deemed to be cheating the Church of its right to mete out punishment. The Church updated this law in 563 to include all who died in suicide. The conflicting views within the Church on "martyrdom" on one side and "suicide" on the other was a source of endless controversy.

There are many concepts within religious organizations arising from the past which still influence adherents. Many religious groups believe that death will reunite one with others, that it can be self-sacrifice or sacrifice on behalf of one's country or a political party, and that it releases the soul from the body. These ideas can support the notion of suicide in spite of, in some cases, a religious condemnation of it.

Things changed again with the Renaissance in the fifteenth century. The insistence that people must be free from slavery led to an increasing focus on individualism. Some people believed that the right to suicide proved that an individual was not a slave, and, therefore, was not "owned" by any state or religion. Individualism influenced people to see themselves as independent of society, and they began to look to their own circumstances and make their own decisions with less fear of Church law. As Church law became less important in individuals' lives, the need to consider who does own one's life was debated. Does one "own" one's life, or do family, friends, state, and God have a stake in it? Do they have enough of a stake to prohibit suicide?

The Age of Enlightenment in the eighteenth century glorified reason as the way to understanding and social order. This change of thinking caused more changes in the views on suicide. The educated came to view suicide as acceptable if it was rational, and unacceptable if it was irrational, which meant looking at individual circumstances. Did the person have enough ability to reason, that is, were they old enough to understand the consequences of what they did? Did they have enough information to make a reasonable choice? Was the suicide rationally in line with the person's best interests?

In 1780, France decriminalized suicide, and other countries followed suit, albeit slowly, so that suicide and attempted suicide were no longer punishable offences. Religious law did not keep pace, but society was no longer as influenced by religious law as it had been.

## RECENT TRENDS

Recent history has generally shown an increase in suicide rates from the 1950s to highs in the 1970s and 80s, then a decline since to a constant, steady level. We don't know the reasons for the increase, the subsequent decrease, or even why the rates are now remaining constant.

In the United States rates for youths fifteen to twenty-four tripled between 1950 and 1993.[16] The increase was largely in the male population. Teen suicides among American males has increased since the 1960s, rising to a peak for white males in 1987 and then declining, and a peak for black males in 1986 and, after 1994, declining. The reduction in the rate in the 1990s is explained by the Center of Disease Control (1998) as being the result of a "lowered substance and alcohol use among the young and greatly increased prescribing of antidepressants to depressed individuals."[17] In spite of the CDC's definite statement, there is much controversy about what influences suicidal behaviours.

We may not find a definitive list of causes for teen suicide, but we can begin to understand it better and trust that, with increased understanding, we can be more effective in offering the teens in our society a more hopeful life.

Scholars who study suicide offer valuable and interesting advice, but it is important to realize that the notion of suicide has evolved, changed, and been modified over centuries to our present view of suicide as an individual act. We now need to consider the historical views around suicide in order to view it as not only the individual act of a teen, but also one that is set in the context of the teen's family, society, and culture.

# TWO

## *Contributing Factors*

*I paint a pretty picture, for all the world to see*
*My smile is big n' brite, we all live happily*
*I don't want to continue, I feel so insecure*
*But my friends are always there, they help me to endure*
*We play this silly game, around the world we go*
*Are people here for real? or will I ever know?*
*I rub my knees 'n' elbows and get up one more time*
*I reach down for my mask, to complete my lonely crime*
*I sing their songs of longing and smile my life away*
*It doesn't get much better. I'm here, but not to stay.*

−T.S.

### FINDING PATTERNS

Studying suicide among teens is overwhelming, like looking for patterns in a storm at sea. If you are in the boat with the waves crashing around you, it seems chaotic, but if you are sitting in a meteorology station measuring winds, tides, and currents, the storm has a pattern that may even be predictable. After interviewing teens in their homes and meeting places across the country, I retreated to my office and studied what they had told me.

I listened to the tapes I had made of our conversations with the hope that patterns would emerge that would illuminate the reasons why they chose to attempt suicide, and help find what factors were important. I wanted to find individual as well as family and cultural patterns. The teens talked about many things, but generally highlighted six areas that concerned them. They spoke of the need to "belong," to have friends and share perspectives of life and death, the importance of family, the need to communicate with someone, the need for a purpose in life, and the power of their emotions. These six perspectives form the structure of the following discussion on teen suicide.

Some literature about suicide separates the influences that teens experience into "predisposing factors," "contributing factors," and "precipitating factors." Here I have combined predisposing and contributing factors and separated precipitating factors, calling them "trigger" events. While this probably doesn't make any difference to most readers, there will be some whose knowledge of suicidal behaviour is precise. I assure those readers that I have included all known factors.

## THE TEENS

I interviewed thirty teens over a period of about a year in many different cities and small towns. As these few vignettes show, they were of varying ages, backgrounds, and personalities.

I put an ad in the "personal" or "information wanted" section of a newspaper which I thought teens would read. In most papers, the ad read:

Teenagers and Suicide
Writer needs interviews with
15–19 yr olds for teen book.
Please call xxx-xxxx

Respondents phoned an answering service and left their names and telephone numbers for me to call back.

Rena was a fifteen-year-old student in grade nine, living at home with her parents and quietly eager to help other teens who were troubled about suicide. She had red-brown hair, brown eyes, an elf-like face. A good student, Rena had loving parents who had lost track of her problems when they became preoccupied when the family moved to a new city. Rena had been sexually abused when she was eight years old by the brother of a friend of hers. He told her it was her fault, that all men would treat her like that, and that she physically invited it because she was pretty. When Rena reached puberty she was confused about her physical appearance at the same time she was upset by the move to a different city and the need to make new friends. At her new school, she was "accused" of being a lesbian – this was considered an insult. Rena didn't know why the other girls started this rumour, only that it isolated her and made life very hard. She didn't know where to go for help, so she tried suicide.

Bruce, now twenty-four, was habitually ignored and rejected by his family. He hit the streets of Vancouver at the age of ten and stayed on and occasionally off the streets and in and out of detention homes until he was eighteen when he went to jail for three years. Prior to leaving home, he had to survive a family that fought all the time, including a father who left home when Bruce was young and who constantly criticized him, probably as a way to hurt Bruce's mother, who in turn used Bruce to hurt her husband. Bruce left them both and "did his own thing," on the streets.

Colleen, in Toronto, was driven to our meeting at the Burger King by her mother. Colleen was trying to deal with parents who cared, but who didn't allow her a chance to make her own decisions; she felt suffocated by the attention. She had made one suicide attempt. Her mother took that attempt seriously and spent hours listening and talking to her. Colleen was one of the rare teenagers I spoke to who felt her parents, or at least her mother, cared.

Family scenarios varied with each teen I interviewed. Some teens had one parent at home and no brothers or sisters; others had both siblings and parents, but no one who they felt cared about them. Some teens spoke of parents who were alcoholic, drug addicted, or workaholic; others had parents who were hard-working, reliable, "Leave it to Beaver" types. Some parents were professionals, others subsisted on welfare. The time the parents spent with their teens didn't seem to have anything to do with whether they worked outside the home or not, whether their jobs took them away for periods at a time, or whether they came home every night.

Most teens were going to high school, but some worked, usually at poorly-paying jobs such as waitressing, dishwashing, or acting. Some liked their jobs. Jake worked two jobs and played drums in a rock band, which gave him satisfaction. Robert liked his acting and film production, Leslie enjoyed her volunteer work with a theater company, and Helen appreciated her job with a fast food restaurant.

I asked about their living arrangements. Most lived at home; some because they were still in high school, others because they couldn't afford to move out. Four lived in foster care, but had emotional ties to their original family. Two were living with their boyfriends, but still talked about their family as the biggest influence on their lives. Nine lived on their own in apartments, but still found their parents' opinions very important.

Mike was tall, dark, with black eyeliner to intensify his brown eyes. His black hair stood eight inches above his head in a punk style with a curl that hung straight down between his eyes and stopped just above his mouth. He wore a cross in his ear as well as other earrings, and – naturally – black clothes. He had a wonderful sense of humour and very warm personality. Mike told me about his struggles to be a part of his family while trying to be independent and make his own decisions. He fought with his parents constantly.

"My mother thinks we get along great, but I don't think we get along at all. I couldn't talk to her. I couldn't tell her my problems. My dad's different – we don't get along at all. They think they're pro-talking, but they're not. My parents called me on Sunday [he'd moved out six weeks prior to our conversation] to yell at me because of my report card. But I don't know. They were always pushing me and pushing me to get really high marks in school. I could if I really tried. But I never tried. I don't know. I never tried hard and they'd always get really upset with me and do things to punish me. Like I'm stuck in the middle of nowhere [in a rural area] and the worst thing they can do is take the car. So they did. I'd lock myself in my room and I'd think about things like that. It just made no sense."

I asked why, if his parents were willing to talk, he wouldn't talk to them.

"They would tell their friends about it. That's one of the reasons I stopped talking to them. I couldn't trust them. My parents have this great imagination. They think that we are really, really close, yet I don't see that at all. I was close at one time to my mother, but never to my father. My father is the kind of guy, who . . . I love baseball. I loved playing it when I was a kid. But being out on a farm where there are no teens around, I was always by myself. My dad would come home on weekends and I'd go up to him and ask him if he would play with me and he'd say no, he wanted to sleep. He never played with me. Never. You know you always see the typical father on TV with his teens. I didn't understand why he wouldn't."

I asked Mike if he thought it was his fault.

"Yes, exactly. We were never close, but my parents always think we should talk to each other. Like, I should like unravel my heart? I can't. I refuse to, because I just don't trust them."

Helen did not have Mike's flamboyance nor his aggressive attitude toward life. We met for coffee in a mall in Winnipeg. She was quiet, even subdued. At nineteen, she worked as a shift manager at a fast-food restaurant, liked her job, and thought she was appreciated there. She lived at home with her mother and father, but never felt that she belonged. "Ever since I've been little I've been sort of a loner, not really having any friends. I never talk to my parents. I can't talk to my mom about anything." Helen's hope was to gradually increase her self-esteem until she could make her own choices and achieve more independence of mind. At the moment I interviewed her, she felt flattened by the aggression in her family and her social group.

The teens I met attempted suicide in many ways. Some had imitated the acts of movie stars and rock singers, and tried suicide in ways they heard about, read about, or invented. Once they had decided on suicide, they saw many ways to do it.

Some wrote poetry to express the emotions they felt at the time. When I read it I could sense the anger, sadness, and depression. Some still felt hopeless, useless. But others were now past that and felt organized, ambitious, competent. It was only when they told me of the past that I could see the pain that went with the confusion of the time.

## FAMILY DYNAMICS

Teens told me they were preoccupied by their relationships with their family. I was impressed and, as a parent, at times horrified by the way many viewed the role of their parents in their lives.

I expected to find teenagers who had little to do with their parents, who were involved with their friends and spent little time at home. I thought that they would tell me their parents were rather nice, but old, and remote from their lives. Instead, they told me that their parents were more important to them than anyone else, that they influenced them more than anyone else. Even when they had left home and were happy, involved with a new loving relationship, they still looked on their parents as a strong influence. Parents mattered.

Most looked on their relationships with their mothers and fathers separately. They didn't think of their parents as a team.

Somehow I had expected the relationships with mothers to be the most important; that their mothers' support and love, or lack of it, would be crucial. But twenty-seven out of thirty of the teens I interviewed told me that they had difficulties with their fathers. They rated him anywhere from four to minus five on a scale of one to ten, where ten indicated a good relationship. Mothers, perhaps, were more consistently supportive, and were rated anywhere from four to nine. Even when their relationship with their mother wasn't good, teens still seemed to be more disturbed by their poor relationship with their father than their poor relationship with their mother.

Why are dads so important? Most teens told me that they wanted their father's approval, that nothing they did was ever good enough for him. Girls were just as demoralized by their father's poor opinions as boys were. It helped if their mother loved and supported them, but it didn't make up for the fact that their father didn't.

Some teens felt that they deserved this negative treatment from their fathers. They felt that they weren't much good, didn't do very well in school, and didn't have many accomplishments. Others had grown past that belief and now felt that they were "good" people with talents and opportunities. They resented the pain their father had put them through: the doubts, the worries, the low self-esteem that they had lived with for years, because, for a time, they had accepted their father's poor opinion of them.

I had a very difficult time listening to these teens tell me how they were treated by their fathers. My father did not always understand me, but he cared and thought I was smart, likable, a little unpredictable, but basically a nice kid. I was twenty years old before I realized that each of his children (six of us) thought he or she was Dad's favourite child. Conveying that attitude to six children was a remarkable feat.

Why is it so hard for so many men to treat their children with respect? None of these teens "deserved" the treatment they got. Twenty-seven out of thirty could have used a different kind of paternal attention. It was difficult to listen to them blame themselves for their fathers' lack of love: "I know I'm not very special. I know I'm not what he wants." This was heart-breaking and I knew that nothing I could say would help. Don't fathers realize the influence they have on their teens?

Helen of Winnipeg spoke of her relationship with her father. "Ever since I've been little my father has always told me I was good for nothing. Ever since I was little. 'Stupid kid.' Stuff like that. From what I found out, I've had a few friends from my childhood try suicide, and they've gone through basically the same thing. I had one friend, her father called her a slut all her life. She finally ended up believing him. I finally believed that I was actually worthless. I'm now trying to believe that maybe I'm not. But it's hard, after hearing my father for so many years."

What does society expect of fathers? Do men know how to be good fathers? Do they know how much they are needed?

The teen years are expensive and it is possible that many fathers withdraw from their families at this time to avoid spending money on their children. They don't remember their own fathers spending so much money on them, and don't see why they should do that for their children. Possibly, when marriages break apart, fathers opt for a new family and turn their backs on the old – an effort to re-invent themselves as a younger, more vital self. The children of previous marriages may be a casualty of this rejuvenation. Perhaps the father is looking for a perfect relationship, one that doesn't include children. This has been described in Larry Frolick's book *Splitting Apart*[1] as an effort to become part of a "perfect couple," the modern myth of the romantic, all-for-love, energetic, successful marriage. If not successful the first time, one may decide to change partners and pursue the "perfect marriage" with someone else – without the "old" children. Instead of working at a marriage partnership, individuals shed old partners to find another who they hope will provide them with an instant, perfect relationship. The children are lost in such a quest.

But the children don't get a new father. Even a stepfather is not usually, for a teen, a replacement father. For most, telling their father that they needed him was impossible. Their relationship was so poor that they thought their father would see any sign of need as a weakness that he should discourage. Perhaps a counsellor or someone their father respects could tell him; maybe another man, a business associate, a friend, a family member. But if a father is determined to leave his children behind, it is impossible for the child to effect much change in the relationship. The relationship isn't, after all, part of the father's plan.

Teens already know that every relationship is different, that there won't be any great rule that magically makes everything okay. Some have fathers who are alcoholics, some are workaholics, and some are so withdrawn that the teens don't think it possible to ever reach them. The problem is, teens who have poor relationships with their fathers probably aren't going to be happy until they figure out some kind of relationship that works, so it is worth it to them to continue to try. Their connection to their fathers was very important, they told me. It influenced everything they did.

## FAMILY PATTERNS

Even though many of the teens I interviewed had different degrees of closeness to their parents and in particular had poor relationships with their fathers, they lived as part of a family dynamic. Patterns in families are many and varied, so it isn't reasonable to think that everyone will fit into neat models, but many will. The following are a few of the common ways that the teens who had tried suicide related to their families. How these relationships influence a teen toward suicide is, of course, not proven. But the fact that the many teens in this study talked about these patterns indicates that such patterns might exist in the lives of other teens vulnerable to suicide.

### The Scapegoat

These teens were blamed for all the troubles in the family. If their parents quarrelled with each other, it was the teen's fault. If their brother was in trouble at school, it was the teen's fault. If there wasn't enough money in the house, it was the teen's fault. While the family was busy blaming the teen, they never looked at the real basis for the problem. Father and mother continued to quarrel with each other and never looked at the real reason they were quarrelling; every fight turned into a fight about the teen. Such teens became used to being found at fault and expected it. After a while, they believed that they were "prone to trouble," that there was something about them that attracted it. They said and did all the "wrong" things and came to believe their family's estimation of them. One teen's family got into the habit of blaming her for many of the family problems, even though outwardly they were fun-loving, intelligent, friendly, hospitable people. At fifteen she was in an accident, hospitalized, and away from her family for eight months. In the hospital, no one blamed her. During this time she realized that she wasn't to blame for much of what went on around her. When she returned to her family she saw what they were doing and somehow, when she knew what was happening, it no longer had the same power over her. She stopped believing them. She simply refused to accept their evaluation of her, which she found liberating. But usually teens do not get this time away to gain perspective and cannot see that they are blameless; they usually adopt the family's beliefs about them.

### The Loser

In this family pattern, the teens were the designated loser in the family, the one who would always fail. The family made it clear that the teens wouldn't do well in school, would never get a good job, would probably end up in jail, and did not have any positive future. They had no expectation that the teens would bring them anything but trouble even though, in some cases, the family could be loving, affectionate, and supportive at the same time. As with the scapegoat, the teens believed their family's assessment of them. Their expectations became self-fulfilling prophecies; because their family thought they couldn't do anything, *they* didn't think they could either. After all, if the people who knew them best and presumably loved them most thought they were losers, then the family was probably right. It amazed the teens in these families how ordinary, everyday living landed them in so much trouble. The family needed to rescue them from themselves all the time; they may have shown affection and love, but they didn't expect the teens to be able to look after themselves, or to be able to solve problems by themselves. These teens were expected to always need the family, and ultimately felt incompetent because of it.

### The Perfectionist

In this instance, the teens' parents expected a perfect child. These teens may have managed to get good grades and meet parental expectations in elementary school, but when they reached high school, their parents' expectations conflicted with their own. Their friends also now had expectations of them, as did their teachers. Family expectations collided with cultural expectations, and perfectionist children could not adequately satisfy all the new demands made of them. They were used to pleasing their parents, but when they tried to please everyone, the stress became too great. It seemed easier to escape in suicide than to fail in life.

These family patterns are not unusual and are easy to slide into. Not all teens are not deeply disturbed by them, but some are. Not all parents who are involved in such patterns are cruel and sadistic, although some are. Parents act out of habit.

How do these family patterns make the teen feel? Useless, incompetent, "bad," confused, rejected, unhappy and, *naturally*, rejected.

Leslie was the first teen I interviewed. She lived with her brother on the top floor of a house owned and occupied below by her parents. Petite and lively, she was passionately committed to helping other teens who were thinking of suicide. She was working on a play about suicide and had returned to her high school to convince the guidance teacher to include suicide in class discussions. Leslie taped our interview on her tape recorder as I taped it on mine.

She told me, "I used to think of my family as a wall. It was everyone against me. They used to blame me for something and I'd say nothing back. It's only recently that I stand up for myself. It used to hurt me a lot to think that these people are my family and they do this to me. But I guess they needed to get their anger out and they put it on me. If something went wrong it was always my fault. After a while I decided I might as well do rotten things because they blamed me anyway. I couldn't lose the respect I didn't have. I used to think highly of myself up to Grade nine and then after that it was like . . . the shits. Sometimes I still think of my family as a wall because sometimes they still all gang up on me."

Janet lived in Calgary with her grandparents. She had been out camping with a girlfriend for two days and missed our first appointment, but was able to catch me before I left for the airport. She talked about her grandparents.

"They weren't accepting me. I wasn't really a person. I was just something there. That's how I felt with them. I couldn't talk to them about anything. They were never really straight with me – like I was real trouble and had to be controlled."

It seems to take some time before the teens realize that their parents' assessment of them was biased and not accurate, and that their own assessment of the relationship might be more real.

## TEENS AND CULTURE

Most of us had a difficult time as teens believing that we were acceptable to the larger social group; that we did belong and were an important part of that group. The social group is one of the teen's most important cultural groups; to feel that we belong among our peers means that we see our place in the culture. Ethnic and religious connections also play a role. Researchers Michael Chandler and Chris Lalonde (1998) point out the strong relationship between teens who see themselves connected to a long tradition in a strong culture and a lower rate of suicide. While there is debate about this, it does seem important that everyone see him or herself as part of a bigger community. Teens who are dancers in their aboriginal feasts and ritual celebrations have a sense of belonging. Teens who have a place in the religious ceremonies of their church also feel a sense of belonging. Both ethnic cultural communities and church organizers often pay attention to the needs of the young people and encourage them to partake in and be a part of the larger organization. Teens try to be accepted by their peers while still holding on to some of their traditional culture.

Different ethnic cultures often contribute to differing world views. Teens may have learned to see the world through the template of their ethnic beliefs and values, and find those values at odds with the popular culture they are also trying to fit into. They may feel appropriate in their own cultural groups, but out of place in the larger society. They may feel a strong conflict between what their ethnic culture teaches and what their teen culture expects. Those who find that the teen culture does not differ dramatically from their ethnic culture will have less difficulty than those who experience great conflicts. Imagine coming from a culture that values virginity, arranged marriages, and separation of the sexes, and trying to fit into a milieu that views sexual activity as causal, self-gratifying, and the inherent right of all young people. Imagine belonging to an aboriginal community where respect of elders is practiced while trying to fit into a teen culture where baiting teachers is considered an indoor sport.

It is the nature of teen culture to resist the established social rules and traditions of the dominant adult culture. Teen culture is by nature a popular culture of resistance.[2] Teens strive to be separate from adults, but for vulnerable teens, the isolation that may ensue from this process creates a sense of loneliness and rejection that they find very difficult to deal with. Although teen culture has a quality of resistance, teens are unlikely to find a sense of belonging and purpose there. It is in the adult culture where teens eventually find acceptance and support. It is the nature of the teen culture to be constantly changing as the larger mainstream culture appropriates the symbols of teen resistance – multiple earrings until multiple earrings are no longer a symbol of teen resistance, skateboarding until skateboarding becomes mainstream. Teen culture is a constantly moving, dynamic, exciting, ever-changing collection of symbols, goals, and ideas. It provides constant tension between wanting freedom in resistance to adult authority and order, and wanting to belong in adult society. The ever-changing teen culture does not provide lasting security not only because of its shifting foci but because eventually the teens grow older. With age, the individual disqualifies them from the culture.

Teens need to find their place in adult society; they need to be securely connected to their culture and feel a sense of belonging to it. Some teens I interviewed felt that they didn't fit into the adult world, and that they were never going to belong there. They felt there were no jobs for them, no place where they could feel at ease. Society wasn't ready for them. No one was moving over to let them into the working world.

Suzanne tried to tell me how hard it was. "Teenagers are the most put-down, unsure. . . . [When applying for a job] you go into an interview room and I always feel so self-conscious. I look around and everyone else is in their twenties. Oh god. There's no possibility for me, you know? 'Cause you haven't really had the experience. But you want the job. Like, you're eager to do it and you're willing to learn. But they don't want that.

"I wish I was older. I wish I could be alone to live my own life, the way I want it. I could, but I'm too young. I can't get a job. I don't have the education. And even though I know I'm ready to do it, I can't. And so I have to put up with being a teenager, you know?"

I asked, "Like a second-class citizen?"

"Yeah. You're not really important."

"So nobody needs you?"

"Not really."

Suzanne was not alone in believing that she would never have a place in adult society. Teens from minority cultures feel this alienation from mainstream adult society very strongly and are intimidated by it. If they can see opportunities within their own culture they have more hope, but many feel there is no place for them in the adult world. It was this feeling of isolation that drove so many to desperation.


### Lack of Intimacy

It amazed me to hear how little intimacy teens had in their families. Most seemed to exist in a world of superficial relationships where caring is expressed as constant criticism. Parents demand better grades at school, different clothes, different friends, different music. The message to the teens is that whatever they are, it isn't good enough. Some parents told them that they criticized because they cared, but the teens didn't believe that. Few thought that their parents were wrong or overly critical, most thought that the parents were right – the teen was a second-class child, not good enough, not smart enough, not mature enough. They did not feel they could sit down and tell their parents, what their problems were. They felt that that would only invite more criticism.

### Abuse

A female teen I interviewed told me I should ask all the teens whether they were sexually abused. Certainly, sexual abuse occurring within the family would affect the teens' feelings of safety, love, and care, as well as their sense of self-worth. I discovered that six of my interview subjects had been sexually abused. If we take one in three as being the national average for women and one in five as the national average for men, that comes within our (unacceptable) national average.

What did surprise me was the incidence of physical abuse. There was a lot more of that than I expected. Most were hit by their parents, some through childhood and others until well into their teen years. What was really startling was that many of them accepted the abuse as being their fault, that somehow they deserved it.

Beth is eighteen years old, pretty, with thick, curly auburn hair. Her family lived in a wealthy district of Vancouver. At the time of our interview, she lived in an apartment with her boyfriend, which she had furnished with old, comfortable easy-chairs and sofas. She made coffee in her clean, tidy, artistically-arranged kitchen. Her new kitten purred at us; Beth put him outside and then told me about her family.

"My father, he was, oh, he was scary. Very scary. Like, we would never talk back to him. And I suppose that's why we never talked. We were so afraid of saying something bad. But when I was about thirteen I started talking back. It was a mistake.

"He hit me. And I hit him back. Then he grabbed me and it was in the kitchen and he picked me up and put me on the counter. I kicked him and called him a bastard and he smacked me and threw me on the floor. I broke his chain that my mom gave him and I always felt bad.

"Funny . . . just before [my first suicide attempt] I had a boyfriend. He was my first boyfriend and my first lover. He'd smacked me around. I was used to it. My mother used to get really abusive, so I was used to it. And every so often he'd rape me, but I thought, well, this is my boy-friend, he just got aroused or something. And it was my fault. And before I went into the hospital I didn't realize how bad that made me feel. But they helped me see it there. Rape is rape. It doesn't matter if he's your boyfriend or not. I seem to attract men that hit me."

Bruce, who had spent his adolescence on the streets, told me: "I stayed in a house in downtown Vancouver. I can't remember the name of it. The corrections officer there was really helpful. He said at any time if I needed him, if I felt like doing something stupid, to call him. He's some-one I know I can trust. He's the only person in my whole life who ever worried about how I feel deep down inside. How I really feel. He made me realize that I could look after myself. Tell your parents to go to hell. Set yourself a pattern and follow it.

"I was never abused as a kid. I got my lickings like everyone else. And I should have gotten a hell of a lot more. Believe me, I should have. I know I was really a hellraiser. I'd bite people and I got lickings for that. When I got older and I'd say to my mom, 'Oh, fuck off,' you know? She used to backhand me right across the face and say, 'Don't ever say that to me again.' It got worse and worse when I was a kid. It seemed that there were arguments and fights all the time."

But Bruce doesn't see that he was abused, that the violence in his family caused the violence in his rebellion. He only sees that he "deserved" to be hit.

Tanya said she was never hit. "For a while when I was three or four, my dad used to smack my mom around. I feel that's sort of where my problems started. Like he lost control and then so did I. He never smacked me around. My sister got it, and my mom, but I never did. That's another thing. See, I was always his precious kid. And no matter what I did I'd get punished and I'd get sent to my room, but I never got hit. And I remember at the time I was never afraid of getting hit because I knew I never would, but now I wish someone would hit me, you know? I want someone to hit me. I want to be hurt, to sort of pay for the wrong things I do. I don't know if that's all related."

Leslie said, "They [her parents] used to hit us when we were younger and we had a lot of trouble with that. My sister ran away from everything."

Mona, eighteen, was independent, self-supporting, and an enthu-siastic, aggressive speaker. We met for lunch in a restaurant in downtown Vancouver.

"Like my jacket?" she asked.

"Love it."

"Bought it with my own money."

"How did you get your clothes before?"

"Stole 'em."

She was happy both with her clothes and with "going straight." Mona had had a brush with the law on a stolen credit card charge and never wanted to be in the hands of the law again. Life was different for her now; she "had it together." She told me about her relationship with her dad. "If he gets mad he starts hitting. But he hasn't hit me in over a year and a half because I told him, 'If you hit me again, I'll charge you with abuse.' My head was ringing 'cause he'd hit me twice on the head and I wasn't going to have that any more. He'd hit me a lot before that. My mom didn't hit me, though. She used to hit me when I was little. She'd say, 'You're a bad kid.' When I was fourteen I hit her back. I said, 'You're a bad mom.' So she said, 'This is where you take over, Daddy. You can take care of the brat from now on.'"

Amy, now babysitting in a suburb of Vancouver, didn't have much luck with her parents. "My dad's really violent. He loves to hit. He hits really well. My mom likes to scream. We used to fight pretty deadly, me and my mom — fist-fight. It was pretty wicked. She'd hit me with whatever she had in her hand. If she was cooking, she'd hit me in the face with a spatula. She'd throw her dinner at me. One time she just about pushed me down the stairs. I got pretty fed up with it and I just close-fisted her and knocked her right on her ass. It made me feel so good. Until my dad got home. And I got it."

Most suffered verbal abuse. They were yelled at, degraded, criticized, told they were incompetent, a loser, a misfit in the family. Sometimes they were told that their birth had wrecked the family, that their parents wished they'd leave. Under these conditions many of them had low self-esteem and considered suicide as a permanent way of leaving.

Sometimes teens felt that they fit into their family, that they were part of it, even when they didn't feel necessary to it. Many of them didn't feel needed and didn't think anyone in the family would really miss them if they were no longer there. They thought they were in the same hole as Helen, the one she was trying to crawl out of. They felt that the ground could close over them at any minute and no one would notice they were gone.

## Isolation

Many had good relationships with their families until they became teens, when suddenly they had their own room, music, friends, timetable. Their families seldom talked to them, seldom listened, and they rarely did anything together – and the teens missed them. They felt lonely, rejected, unreal. They needed their parents to tell them they were okay, that they belonged, were important, necessary. They needed them to be part of their lives. Often the teens and their parents got into circular patterns of action and reaction. The teens wanted to spend more time with their friends, so their parents reacted by spending less time with them; the teens reacted in turn by not being around when the parents were home, so the parents criticized the way the teens spent their time. The teens didn't tell their parents about school, so the parents stopped asking, then the teens thought their parents didn't care and their grades went down, which their parents then hassled them about. Soon many teens lived their lives separate from their parents, even if they still resided in the same house. They still needed their parents' attention, concern, and love so they could feel worthwhile and secure, but everything the teens and parents did seemed to drive them further apart, leaving the teens feeling isolated and lonely.

Social isolation is one characteristic of teens considering suicide; teens who spend a lot of time alone in their rooms or away from home. This isolation increases until they spend very little time with anyone, including the people who used to be their friends. They don't yell, scream, argue, or demand attention; they just quietly withdraw from family and friends, interacting with no one.

If they lived outside of urban areas, the teens I spoke to found it easier to be isolated. It can be difficult to find networks of friends in rural settings where people live several miles from each other. The teenage years can be marked by periods of intense loneliness; these feelings can be exacerbated when no one else is around.

But loneliness also occurs in the city and when there are people around. A teen can be in the middle of a crowded school cafeteria and still feel that he or she is the only person in the world. When engulfed in this loneliness, teens often do not try to reach out to anyone. They learn a way of dealing with rejection: they withdraw. It may not be a way to solve the problem, but it relieves such feelings and allows them to function temporarily.

### Underlying Family Patterns

Teens' desire for suicide comes out of their interactions with their culture, family, and their own character. There is not a great deal of research on family dynamics around suicide, but there are indications that some family patterns are more likely to lead teens to ideas of suicide than others. Scenarios that can contribute to this are ones in which:

- there is a warm and possessive mother and a distant and hostile father;
- the teen is singled out as the troublemaker, the scapegoat, the expendable one who is not accepted by the family as he is;
- the teen is compared to negative models; he is "just like grandpa," "just like your father," or "just like" someone the family doesn't accept;
- the family tries to keep members from seeking intimacy with non-family members;
- there are long-term patterns of depression, alcoholism, and drug abuse;
- there are anger and communication issues between mother and father;
- the family is inflexible; any change in status, achievements, jobs, earning power, or goals is interpreted as threatening the family.

Not all these symptoms necessarily occur in one family, but to the extent that any one of the symptoms of family dysfunction contributes to the teen's feelings of inadequacy and his conviction that he is not accepted by his family, they contribute to his desire for escape — a feeling that can be manifested in suicide. Rejection, even if it is only perceived, is very difficult for teens to deal with.

Teens may respond to rejection from their parents by talking only about what the parents want to talk about. They may seldom bring up their own subjects for discussion. Of the teens I interviewed, some parents responded to their teens' withdrawal and isolation with criticism, ridiculing, name-calling, telling them they were stupid, lazy, worthless, and no-good. This made the teens feel even more unloved. Some parents physically abused their teens, although this usually happened less often as the teens got older. Some parents had an ongoing hostile attitude towards their teens that resulted in continual put-downs, locking them out of the house, turning off porch lights while they were still out, omitting to set a place for them at the table, arranging family outings without them, and talking about them to others when the teens were present as if they were invisible. In these situations, the teens felt powerless; they usually saw no way of changing the pattern except escape.

Sometimes the put-downs were more subtle. Some parents told their teens what their faults were and then said they were only "teasing." The teens felt attacked and then confused because they were accused of over-reacting. But even teasing is a form of aggression. The teens' initial reaction was usually correct; they were being attacked.

Sometimes parents committed small, insidious, repetitive acts that resulted in teens feeling incompetent. One teen's mother made her bed and straightened her room every day. Wasn't that "nice" of her? But the teen felt that her privacy was being invaded, and that her mother was telling her that she was still a little girl who needed looking after.

These kind of subtle behaviours made teens feel uncomfortable. They knew there was something wrong, but they couldn't define it. Nothing their family did seemed "serious" enough to warrant such an emotional reaction on their part. Essentially, they were taught not to trust their own emotions.

But, very often, their feelings were correct. Subtle, small, and constant pressures can cause big problems in a teen's self-image. For instance, if a teen asks a parent a question and the parent simply doesn't answer, the teen feels unimportant, invisible. It helps to know that *most* people would feel degraded in that situation, that such a reaction is valid.

Many teens automatically tense when a parent says, "Because I love you, I want to tell you. . . ." or, "It's for your own good." These remarks are usually a cover for criticism. Teens need to know it is quite okay to feel hurt; it is quite okay to trust their own reactions.

For some teens a moment of realization came when they determined that no matter how many times they tried suicide, they could not control their parents' ability to care about them. This was the time they started building a life of their own. It was very difficult to do and often only possible when they had a strong love for another, or a strong network of friends. But some managed this with very little support.

## Siblings

Teens told me that their relationships with their brothers and sisters ranged from very cold to very warm. However, these relationships didn't seem to make much difference to how they felt about themselves. They didn't necessarily believe their brothers' or sisters' opinions, even when the opinions were positive. The problem may be that teens don't feel a lot of support from their brothers and sisters because they don't see them as powerful people in their lives. The siblings may also be suffering from a difficult family pattern similar to their own.

I asked if anyone else in their family had tried suicide. No one who talked to me had lost a brother or sister to suicide, but some knew a family member or relative who had either attempted or committed suicide. Some sources suggest that suicide is three times more likely if there is a family history of suicide, which is commonly accepted as a risk factor.[3] This is considered by some psychiatrists as significant in whether or not a teen chooses suicide, but the teens I interviewed didn't tell me that thoughts of their relatives' deaths worried or influenced them, so I can't state that such a loss made them more likely to try suicide.

## Sex

Many teens reported that no one in their family spoke to them about sex. There were no discussions about the practical, real facts of life, nor about sexual feelings, nor about how they should act in particular sexual situations. Even now, in the supposedly frank times of today, some found themselves handicapped by inadequate sexual knowledge. Some teens didn't know how to handle the sexual pressures they felt, and got involved in sexual activity before they could really make a reasoned decision about it. When discovered, many teens were accused of sexual promiscuity, of sleeping around; they were called "slut" and "whore" by their parents, usually without justification, which made them feel hurt and bewildered. Sometimes, parents had their own sexual issues; some were unsure of their own sexuality, and some had affairs or casual sexual alliances that they tried to hide from their teens. When teens hit puberty some parents projected their worst fears about sexual activity onto the teen and made accusations. Most of the teens who reported this situation gave up trying to prove their innocence and ironically went looking for sexual experience. Movies and television make sex seem like a romantic idyll or a sport. Yet teens learned fast that sexual experience can be confusing, painful, humiliating, and even physically dangerous.

It always amazes me that we somehow expect teens to know all about sex. We teach them how to add, subtract, and spell but we rarely give much information on such an important subject as sex. Some teens I spoke to had no information and little encouragement to become aware of their own sexuality. In spite of the books that tell us we should all be more open and honest about sex, teens are still told to ignore their sexuality, pretend their bodies haven't changed, that their feelings haven't matured, that they are still little girls and boys. And somehow, magically, everyone will understand sex.

The conflict this created in the teens I interviewed very often added to their stress, but seemed to increase their inclination to suicide only when they couldn't talk about it with their parents, or when the conflicts around sexuality included orientation. The designation of gay or lesbian still carries a great deal of prejudicial behaviour and abuse, and teens generally are very reluctant to disclose a homosexual orientation. However, it is not the orientation that is the problem, but the subsequent social isolation and persecution.

## Peers

*I have built around me*
*a secret glass house*
*I need to look at the world*
*which cannot touch me*
*There is no entrance*

– B.B.

Friends are vital. The teens I interviewed couldn't think of living without their friends. They all seemed to need one intimate, close friend who was willing to accept them, listen to their troubles, and believe in them. But this was what they said they needed, not what they had. Few had close friends. Most would refer to someone as a friend even if they didn't know each other well but perhaps because they went to the same school, hung around the same mall, or were members of the same club or sports team.

Suzanne was blonde and fifteen years old, but she looked a few years older. She invited me into her parents' split-level home in Calgary. We sat at the dining room table, restricting our conversation to school subjects whenever her father or mother came into the kitchen, then switching back to talking about suicide when they left. Suzanne said she had never talked about suicide with her parents. I wondered what she told them I was doing in their house.

Suzanne said that friends forced her into a social role that she wasn't sure she liked. "In the summer you can be yourself. [It was July when we were talking.] Like, I don't like hanging around my school friends in the summer. I already have a best friend. I have my out-of-school friends. I become myself, really. When you're going to school it starts off okay in September. People say, 'Wow, have you ever changed.' Then you fall into the role. You fall into little social cliques. What's cool. What's in."

I suggested that she had to adapt to survive in the school system.

"Yeah," she said with surprise. "I'm really easy to get along with at school. I make friends, not really friends, but acquaintances, really quick. But you have to learn how to act like no one, like an empty role, not real. I always find that you can't really say what you feel."

I asked her why.

"I'm always scared that people won't care. That you're just going to say something that really is bothering you and they'll just laugh at it. Because they've done that. They've just laughed. 'Don't be stupid!' You have to keep your opinions to yourself. You have to be able to laugh, be cool, flippant, don't care. You have to know how to make other people laugh, too.

"Last year I got put through it [ridiculed] and I tried to explain to the people I thought were my friends, 'Listen, don't do that to me. It really *bothers* me.' And they wouldn't understand. 'Oh, it's just a joke. So what?' Like they can be cruel, and then pretend they were funny."

Helen, nineteen, told me that she had only one friend during the period of her life when she was thinking about suicide. "But I couldn't talk to her. She didn't understand. She was going through a rough time herself. She'd have asked me if I was crazy if I tried to tell her. So I just kept it to myself.

"I don't expect anything from people. I try not to expect anything because I've made friends before and I've trusted them and they've ended up hurting me. The way I feel, I can't trust anybody but myself.

"Friends don't talk about suicide. They know it's out there, but they don't talk about it. It's like a taboo. A weakness."

Leslie told me what it was like for her.

"I wish someone could have talked to me. I'd have paid money to have someone talk to me, like *look* at me, not at the picture I was painting for them. It [life] was too much of a game. Even now, some of my friends don't seem to realize how serious it was. Maybe they'll talk easier now, but suicide's too quiet a subject. Teenagers mention it. They say, 'Yeah, it's my parents . . .' and this and that . . . but they don't say, 'It's because I don't feel loved.'

"When my friends talked about suicide, they said, 'Let's all get really drunk and kill ourselves. That'll solve everything.' We'd go through the motions of getting really drunk and say, 'Let's do it.' But I don't know what made us stop. If they were going to jump I'd certainly have grabbed their hands and gone with them. We just didn't. We never talked about what we were feeling, just talked about life being lousy and we should get more drunk."

Some of the teens I interviewed had friends who really cared. They may not have known how to talk to them about their problems or even how to listen, but they were the ones who cared about the teen when no one else did. Some did know how to talk and met as a kind of support group over pizza once a week to talk about anything that was on their minds. But most did not have this kind of close association with friends.

One of the jobs of a teen is to begin the process of separation from the family. It's a preparation for independence and a family of one's own. Friends are very important during this process, and in the teen years, necessary. It is usual for teens to form strong friendships outside the family, and such friendships are a significant part of moving away from the family. Many teens transfer their affections from family to a friend, a boyfriend or a girlfriend, and give that relationship the difficult task of satisfying their need for affection, understanding, and emotional support.

With many of the teens I interviewed, friends were the rescuers. After Leslie tried to hang herself, she stayed in her room and no one in her family bothered to check on her.

"I stayed in my closet for three days. I thought that I wouldn't commit suicide, like suicide would be my fault. I'd just die of starvation, that would be natural. My brother's schedule was different from mine and he didn't know I was in the closet. I just stayed there.

"After three days, my girlfriend came over and she found me. It just blew her mind. She was just crying. She got me out of the house. She pulled me out of the closet and she put me in her car and took me to a doctor. By then I was a mess.

"My friend drove me to the doctor's and the doctor wanted to send me to a counsellor, but I ran out of there. I ran back to the car. I guess he [the doctor] tried to get my parents, but I'm not sure if he ever did because they never said anything about it. My girlfriend took me to some friends' place, Mike and Jason. She was really confused and crying and she said, 'She won't talk to me. Please, you've got to help her.' I was laughing and they were looking at me. I had already cut off the circulation to parts of my body and I was just skinny, you know, and horrible. I just sat there. I was just sitting there still thinking childish things except there were people I kind of recognized. And then Jason gave me a hug. All of a sudden, I realized what was going on. I was looking at myself and my arms and everything and I was crying. They saved me, really."

Many were rescued from the consequences of an overdose by a friend. Beth, eighteen when I interviewed her, sixteen when she tried suicide, told me that her friend helped her.

"My parents went away that weekend and they said, 'Okay, we're going to trust you. We're going away. You can stay here by yourself.' I said, 'Okay. You can trust me.' And I set out to really impress them because I didn't want to go goof off or anything. I don't know why it happened. All I know is I started drinking and I started taking some of my mom's pills and I don't remember half of it.

"We lived on the lake and I went traipsing around the lake, for heaven's sake. I remember parts of that walk, but nothing else. All I know is what my friends told me. I guess I made all these phone calls to them. And the ambulance came to pick me up because my friend, my boyfriend at the time, was freaking out. And I said, 'No, I won't go.' So the ambulance couldn't take me. And my other friend, the boy I live with now, he came over and he's going, 'Mike, what are you doing sitting there crying on the steps?' And he said, 'Beth, she's in the house. She locked herself in the house and she's trying to kill herself.' And Jim goes, 'What?' And he tries the front door and it was locked and he walks around to the back door and it's wide open. So he comes in and he convinces me to go back with the ambulance. I didn't even know what I was doing at the time. I wanted to write something down to my parents, but it all hit me so quickly.

"My parents were up at Penticton when I went to the hospital [in the Vancouver area]. Then Jim sat and waited for me. The hospital had to have a relative sign some papers so they called my grandparents. The next morning I went home to them. They had called my parents. I felt really lousy because my parents came home and I ruined their weekend."

Her friends saved her during a difficult and traumatic time, but Beth sees that suicide attempt as an "inconvenience" to her parents.

Teresa used her friends as family. "One of my friends' mother is really great. I can call her at any time, even four in the morning and she's wide awake and ready to listen. She's really great. I've gone to her a bit and we'll talk. I go over to their place for dinner once in a while."

I suggested that she had gone out and found her own support system.

"Yep. I had to. It wasn't being offered anywhere. You pretty well have to go out and find someone. People aren't going to stand there with open arms and say, 'Come on here,' and all this. No one does this any more. Everyone's too afraid of getting involved.

"Nobody wants to get involved in someone else's problems. So Mrs So-and-So has a problem kid. That's her problem, not mine. That's the way people are. That's where a lot of people are going to be really screwed up. No friends. Nobody to care."

Sometimes it's the sudden absence of the best friend that leaves the teen vulnerable to suicide. Daniel's girlfriend had troubles of her own at exactly the wrong time in Daniel's life.

I met Daniel, seventeen, on the wharf in Halifax. He was blond, broad-shouldered, and seemed confident. We sat in the sunshine and talked for so long that my face was sunburnt for days. He was the youngest of five boys. His father deserted the family when Daniel was four, and his mother, a waitress, supported the family. Daniel had worked since he was thirteen and had managed to overcome a learning disability and stay in the academic program at school. He did not get along well with his older brothers, but had a good relationship with his mother, though none at all with his father. Daniel relied a lot on his friends.

At fifteen Daniel had been taking medication for depression and knew it wasn't working.

I asked him how he knew.

"How can I tell? You know how I can tell the most? Sleeping patterns. If I was happy, I could sleep. If I wasn't, I couldn't. If I was happy, I wanted to eat. If I wasn't, I didn't. So I called the doctor about three weeks later. So they took me down and they gave me this new blood test and they found that I didn't have enough medication and it wasn't working. For another two weeks they debated on what they were going to do and things at that point had become very disastrous.

"My girlfriend's father is an alcoholic. He'd gotten the drift of where I had been and why I was there [in the hospital's psychiatric ward]. His attitude was, 'He's not all there. He's sick. Don't be around him.' One night he began to beat her.

"She told me, 'Whatever he says or whatever he does to me, I won't turn my back on you.' She told me that one day, and the next night she said she couldn't see me any more because of her father. And I was feeling really, really terrible. The only thing that had really brought me around more than anything was her. I was happy with her. When she wasn't around I wasn't happy.

"I had this friend who was a drug pusher. So I went to him and I bought a bottle of amphetamines.

"At that point when I left the hospital the second time, it was the social worker and psychiatrist's recommendation that I not return home because of my grandmother [who had constantly told him he was worthless], that it was not a good environment. My employer at the pizza shop told me I could live at her house. So I moved in there. That was not a problem to me. I liked it there. There was no one at home. I took the amphetamines and lay down. I remember waking up three or four days later, after I'd been in a coma.

"My boss had come home to pick up some records or something like that and she usually checked to see where I was. She had knocked on the door and I didn't answer, so she opened the door and she couldn't wake me up so she called the ambulance.

"My girlfriend . . . I hadn't seen her. I refused. I said, 'Just let me lie here and die.' I didn't eat. I had ivs. It was about three or four weeks before I decided to eat. Matter of fact, my girlfriend *had* come back to see me. Her father had picked her up and thrown her out of the house. She, in turn, got hold of my mother and my mother gave her a place to stay. My girlfriend had come down to see me and she told me what happened. Like, she hadn't let me down. I just didn't know that. It kind of changed my attitude toward things again."

Daniel's will to live at that point depended on his relationship with his girlfriend. She was the only friend he felt he had, the only one who cared for him. And he could not stand, right then, to lose her. Another friend, his boss, had saved him.

It is important for teens to have good, strong friendships. They told me that often it was very difficult to make friends with adults, that there is a great divide, the "them" – adults – on one side, and the "us" – teens – on the other.

Leslie had definite ideas on this. "When you're a teenager, you're not satisfied with anything. You're so uncomfortable. Everything is so new to you. You're right in the middle of young and old. You've got responsibilities, but nobody needs you.

"Society says to teenagers, 'Get lost for ten years. Come back when you have experience.'

"There's such a prejudice against teenagers, like they mean trouble. When you walk down the street people will cross [to the other side]. When people do that it makes me feel so low. When three teenagers walk down the street, people clutch their bags. And when you go and sit next to a person on the bus, they get up and move. My friends and I feel real bad about that. We don't forget that. We take this to heart. We generalize it, 'All adults this – and all adults that,' but that's so wrong because that's what they're doing to us."

Jake, eighteen, was a rock drummer in Toronto. He lived with his mother and visited at his father's apartment. He worked two jobs besides his drumming job. He told me, "No one seems to take teens seriously, including other teens. No one takes teenagers' pain seriously. They put it down. Other teens put it down. Negate it. Say, 'Oh, well, you only failed a grade, one grade. What's the big deal? I failed four. I mean, what are you worried about?' Well, it doesn't matter if you did something worse, or better. This problem worries me. That's what no one seems to accept. That it worries me. It overwhelms me. Everything overwhelms me at this point. I think we [society] don't care enough."

Many teens told me that on numerous occasions they had tried to talk to an adult about their problems. Most saw adults as more capable of helping them when they were in trouble than their friends. Adults seemed more powerful, more able to change the teens' lives. But often adults did what Jake says they do, chided their pain, told them it was nothing. Alternatively, when the teens tried to talk to adults about a topic less serious than suicide, the adults didn't listen, so the teens were afraid to talk about something as dire as killing themselves.

Few were as independent as Daniel, who in some ways is a street kid, although he is cultured and educated and never in trouble with the law. He is so independent that he was able to move past the adults who tried to put him down, past the crisis-line worker who dismissed him, and found a good psychiatrist who did help him. Very few of the teens I interviewed could persist until they found an adult who would help. It seems amazingly difficult for teens to find an adult who will listen. Many told me of feelings of isolation, as if "being a teenager" means it is forbidden for adults to talk to them, or listen to them, or spend any time with them. So teen friends become very important and often the only ones who will listen.

## Violence

The tragic deaths of teens in several high schools in North America at the hands of other students is a reminder of the threat of violence in teens' lives. Bullying at school has become part of teen culture in some areas, and students have been driven to suicide by their fears of physical violence from other students. Bright, affectionate students have left notes to their grieving families naming the bullies at their school who had been tormenting them. Threats and intimidation have become, in some areas, a "normal" part of teen life. Teenaged girls at a high school swarm victims to beat and kick them; disenfranchised and dissatisfied young men bring guns to school to "get even." The need to separate from adults, to have a teen culture that is independent of adults, contributes to the conspiracy of silence that protects bullies and promotes violence. It is hard for teens to betray the bullies to adults and risk social isolation for doing so. It may seem easier to simply escape from it all; many choose suicide.

## Music

Does music aimed at young people cause suicide? Some popular music contain themes of chaos, desperation, and powerlessness, and definitely do *not* advocate hope. Still, it is a big leap to suggest that songs about hopelessness have a direct link to teens taking their own lives. Many genres of music, including country, folk, opera, and blues, tell stories of suicide and despair, and in fact, some argue that such songs actually relieve despair by acknowledging it. Vulnerable teens, who already have formed the intention to die, may use music to help create the mental state that allows them to more readily try suicide in the same way they might use alcohol to reduce their inhibitions so that they are more likely to try it. But it is not music itself that motivates teens to suicide, but the combination of numerous factors: a sense of hopelessness, a lack of organized support, a lack of a sense of place and purpose in the culture, the threat of bullying and violence, and the very transient nature of teen culture. It would be easy to blame music because then all that would be necessary to curb suicide would be to restrict it. But it isn't nearly that simple.

## Imitative and Cluster Suicide

Heroes and celebrities can influence teen behaviour. When someone like a rock star dies by suicide, troubled teens are more likely to choose suicide in imitation of that death.

Teens have been driven to respond to a celebrity killing himself in what are referred to as cluster suicides – a phenomenon where many teens die in a concentrated period of time in a way imitative of the celebrity. Sometimes it doesn't even have to be a celebrity; a "normal" person might die in a spectacular way that grabs the imagination of teens. Kiyoko Matsumoto, a nineteen-year-old student, died by jumping into a volcano in Japan in 1933; over the next several months three hundred children did the same.[4] Clusters can be teens who are unrelated or do not know each other, but who are influenced by the same event, or they can be groups of teens who know each other and make a pact to die together. The cluster phenomenon that can follow a celebrity suicide is more likely to occur in teens than in other age groups, and appears more frequently when teens glorify the celebrity death, and the media romanticizes or dramatizes it. There are guidelines which ask the media to report suicides in an academic and non-dramatic manner in order to prevent cluster suicides.[5] For the most part, the media is responsible and does adhere to such guidelines, which can make a difference in the number of suicides that follow a celebrity's.[6]


### PERSPECTIVE

One of the most difficult things for someone who is not suicidal to understand is how people who decide to end their lives view the act as reasonable. It is also hard to understand that teens may not view death as final. The way teens view their own lives is often not clear to those who love them. We need to try to see teens from their perspective, understand what they are going through, before we can be of any use to them. I asked all the teens I interviewed what happened in their lives to make suicide look like a reasonable option.

Many thought of death as an escape where they would finally be safe. They thought they would *feel* better when they were dead, that death was a temporary state where they could hide in safety for a time. Sometimes they thought that in death they would be able to watch the activities of their family and friends, or that they would be able to comment on what they were doing and how they were feeling.

For some a moment came when they understood that death is in fact final. Suddenly they understood that they would not come back, there would not be a fairy-tale ending: they would not be part of the life they left behind. For some this realization shook them into taking sober responsibility for their own happiness. Often, this didn't occur until the pressures and pain slackened and they had a refuge – a friend's house, an aunt's place, the hospital, a safe environment where they could recover and begin to feel better about themselves.

Suzanne said, "The psychiatrist figures that with everything . . . I just couldn't take myself any more. The first time they figured I was rebelling and it was a call for help. I needed to talk to someone. But the second time, I just couldn't cope. I was really letting my parents down and myself down and the world down.

"The first time I wrote poems before I did anything and I showed them to my mother. She thought they were very nice. They were interesting. She tried to analyze them herself. Some of them were about death. Most of them were analogies like the sun slipping below the horizon, broken glass. My mom thought they were about my boyfriend leaving me, but they weren't.

"I thought death would be like falling asleep. There'd be nothing. But I wouldn't have to put up with what was going on any more. I wouldn't have to keep hurting people and I wouldn't have to keep hurting inside. That's all I knew. I didn't think I was going to go to heaven or anything. I was happy with that. Going to sleep was okay. Then I wouldn't have to do anything. People wouldn't expect so much of me. I wouldn't expect so much of myself. I could stop going around pretending I was happy all the time, doing what everyone else wanted. I'd just be myself. It would just be like black. No dreams. Nothing. I wouldn't have to do anything or see anyone. I never felt that I'd float over my body, have my soul set free or anything. No. Just black.

"I never thought I'd fail the suicide. It was difficult."

Leslie, eighteen now and enthusiastic, energetic, and keen to have me help other teens, told me what life had been like for her. "I used to shoplift when I was twelve. We were better off then [her parents had more money] and I used to have money in my purse, but I stole things I didn't need. I knew I was going to get caught. And I wanted to. I went home and got into trouble and that was it. I went home and it was like, 'You're bad. You've destroyed our family name.' The family name! That was the most important thing. I couldn't believe it. I didn't do it [shoplift] after that because I thought, 'Well, that isn't the way to go. What is the way to go? How do you cry for help around here?' So I used to get caught at a lot of things at home. I used to bring booze home and leave it in obvious places and I'd get caught and they'd say, 'You're even worse than we thought. We've lost all respect for you.' And I said, 'That's okay. I've lost all respect for you, too. Can we talk?'"

Leslie tried many ways to get attention from her parents but was met with constant rejection. A few months previously, everything had become too much. She had an interview with the school counsellor in the afternoon. She sat in front of the counsellor crying; the counsellor criticized her grades and told her to stop trying to manipulate her with tears. Leslie went home. "My boyfriend called and said it was all over. I hung up the phone and walked into my bedroom. It was like there was so much pain I had to get away from it. Like I thought I was dead anyway, my mind was dead, my body might as well be dead too. I hung myself, but the cord broke. So I wasn't dead. And it was like God didn't want me either. No one wanted me. My mother had told me that, like, my grandma and grandpa died within a month of each other when I was about five, and my mother said it was better for grandma. Like there was no more pain for her. She was with God. She was in heaven. I thought it would be good for me. And then not even God wanted me.

"My only other option [than suicide] was to talk to someone and I wasn't good at that at that time. There was no way that I could just release it all without help. There was no way I could do that after seventeen years. I tried the counsellor and that didn't work. I couldn't talk to my parents. I wrote in my diary. To go see a psychiatrist meant lots of money [not necessarily, but Leslie thought it cost money], and people saying 'Why do you want to go see a psych? Are you crazy? What's wrong with you?' I would have loved to go see a psychiatrist, if I had the money and the guts.

"I thought about the crisis centre once, but looking for the phone number was, you know, too much. I called Zenith 1234, but I think that was for child abuse. That was the only number I knew because I remembered it from the television commercials. So I phoned them and they said, 'What area are you?' And I said, 'Vancouver.' And they said, 'Can you hold on a minute?' and that blew me away. Hold on a minute? I was crying when I was on the phone. I hung up.

"After I didn't complete suicide, that must have been the lowest point. And then things got better. I started to realize why I do things, where all my feelings spawn from. I started to feel comfortable with my own emotions. Then I could start to relate to other people. I started to get my self-confidence back. It's only been four months. I've changed a lot in four months. I think so differently. The thing is, I haven't forgotten what I've done. I don't wish to forget because I want to learn from it. But when I look back I can't believe that things could get so bad. I'd like other people to know that things can get bad. When it does get that bad, go get somebody to listen to you, to talk to. I don't think I could ever turn my back on anybody now. Not since I've been there."

Many teens told me how problems seemed to pile up on each other until they had absolutely no idea how to deal with them. They saw nowhere to go, no one to talk to. Suicide looked like an escape. It didn't necessarily appear to them to be the end to life.

Bruce tried to cope with increasing problems when he was very young. He first tried suicide when he was thirteen. "I came home and my dad wanted to see me. He wanted to take me to Kamloops and my mom didn't want me to go. My mom was living with this guy. I was feeling pretty shitty. My mom always had lots of pills hanging around. Pills were my favourite things. I loved to take pills. They blanked you out.

"I came up from downstairs in our house. I'd taken lots of pills and I grabbed a pair of scissors and tried to stab myself. My sister twisted my arm and knocked me down the stairs. The ambulance came and they took me to hospital. They pumped my stomach and kept me overnight. I didn't tell anyone about the pills, but my sister had seen all the pill bottles lying around. They didn't really do anything in the hospital. They gave me a medication that made me throw up. The doctor said, 'Why did you do this?' And I said, 'No reason.' Four hours later my mother and her boy-friend picked me up and took me home. That was about it.

"I think that I was really asking for help. I've been to quite a few doctors, psychiatrists, now to find out what was going on. I think at that time I was trying to get my point across – 'Listen, you guys. I don't want any more of this shit. I don't want it any more!' Finally I just said to my parents, 'Piss off. You guys fight on your own. I'm butting out.'

"When I tried suicide I thought the problems would go away. There would be no problems. If you don't like something, you get rid of it, right? There'd be nothing more to cause pain. 'You guys [his parents] won't go away so I will. I tried to run away from you and live my own life [on the streets] but you wouldn't let me. Why do you keep bringing me back to this place? I don't want to be here.' All the time my parents were dragging me in the front door, I was saying, 'Don't do this. I don't want to be here. Let me go.' I was there, how long? – four hours, five hours? – and then I was out the back and on my way again.

"At thirteen I thought of suicide as 'going away,' not really dying. But after a while I came to respect death.

"But then I tried suicide again. I figured this [living on the streets, on booze and drugs] was going to be my life. And if this was it, I didn't want it. So I took a Coke can and ripped it in half and cut my wrists. Maybe I didn't want to die. Maybe I just wanted to talk to somebody. That's when I went to S Centre [Juvenile Detention]. The RCMP took me to the hospital. They fixed me up and left me in a padded cell for the night.

"Later, when I was in jail, I come to grips with reality. I seen somebody die. The guy in the next cell killed himself and I seen them take him out. I thought, 'When I die that's probably what I'm going to look like.' I seen him lying there and he wasn't moving. He was just lying there and his eyes were open and he wasn't moving. He looked peaceful and all unconcerned, you know.

"I realized that you can't get up from this and walk away. So suicide went out of my head."

Suzanne was twelve when she first tried suicide. "Before, I was having a lot of problems with my parents. I didn't feel like I belonged in my family. I was so different from everyone else. That's why I was so glad to go on the holiday with my friend and her parents. But I got into trouble on that holiday. I lost my virginity. I lost all my pride. I wasn't sexually assaulted, I co-operated, but I wasn't mentally ready for it. I mean, the guy didn't give a shit. It was a one-night stand for him. My virginity was the only thing I really had left and I lost it; and I was twelve."

Suzanne took an overdose of thirty-eight Tylenol pills. Her friend didn't want her to die and persuaded her own parents to take Suzanne to the hospital. Suzanne's parents never did know about this attempt.

"Once you try suicide, then you think about it. It's easier to do the next time. [She spoke softly, slowly, remembering what it was like.] People who haven't tried it can think. But thinking and doing are different things.

"So it was really easy for me to try it again. Like a habit . . . like, 'Try it, see if it works.' But I didn't really want it to work. I just wanted somebody to listen. So I just was thinking and thinking and I OD'd and my last thought was what if Dad comes home and I'm not dead yet, he'll have to stop it. He came home and he stopped it. I haven't tried it since. The thought's there when something happens. People can do it [attempt suicide] over the dumbest things, but to them it's most important.

"I still wanted to try suicide. I didn't know what to do. Like, should I leave a note? I just wanted to be alone. Running away occurred to me. But I didn't do that.

"Now it's easier to deal with my feelings. One time I got out the razor blade and I sat there and I wanted to do it. But I couldn't. I felt like I could always make life better. Like I survived before. Maybe I can do better this time. You sure don't like yourself when you're thinking about suicide. And you think that other people don't like you."

I asked if she thought about whether her parents would miss her when she was gone.

"You don't think about that. Just don't think about that. I wrote poems and they were really sad. I still had one girlfriend who really cared about me, but no one else cared. I had a boyfriend, but he didn't really care about me. I'd go to school and then come back to my room, but I kind of wanted it that way, you know?

"Once you have the idea in your head, it's something you can't get out. When you see a bottle of pills, you think, 'Why don't you take them? It'll all be over. It'll all vanish.'

"I feel like I can handle myself better now. Like, I can handle my emotions. I can deal with the thought of suicide. I can sit there with a razor blade in my hand for an hour, just thinking and come to the conclusion that, well, maybe I should just wait and see what happens. See if things will get better."

Teresa looked at death a little differently.

"I tried the razor blade about four times. Then a friend got me her grandpa's nitroglycerine pills. That just about did it. I did that [tried nitroglycerine tablets] at a party and they took me to the hospital. My mother never found out about it. I wouldn't give them my name. I had no ID. And I wouldn't tell anybody at the hospital who I was. So they just cleared up the nitroglycerine problem and sent me on my way.

"I tried to jump in front of a car once, but I'm scared of cars and I couldn't do it. A big semi came along and it would have been perfect, but I couldn't do it."

I asked her if she thought about how the driver would feel.

"No, not at all. I never thought about the effect on anybody else, really.

"I thought about what it would be like after I died. My parents would be sobbing at the funeral, saying, 'We should have talked to her when we had the chance. Now it's too late.' I'd be sitting there laughing and saying, 'I told you so.' Not really watching the funeral but an 'out of body' experience."

I asked her if she saw death as final.

"No, it didn't really strike me that once I'm dead, I'm not coming back. It didn't strike me as that final. It would be like I could be watching the funeral and I could be laughing at it."

"When did you see death as final?" I asked.

"When I tried the Anacin and Coke. I was hoping to God it was going to be final so I could get out of this life. I was hoping it was going to be slow and painful too so I could say, 'Look, Mom and Dad. Watch me suffer. There's nothing you can do about it.'

"When I woke up the next morning it was, 'Shit! It didn't work!' I blamed myself because it didn't work. Which was stupid. I was furious with myself for weeks because I didn't do it right. I was a failure that way, too. I couldn't even kill myself properly. What can I do right? I can't even kill myself. By that time [she was seventeen], death was definitely lights out.

"After the Anacin and Coke time I realized that I wasn't getting anywhere trying suicide. I decided I was alone. My parents didn't give a damn about what I was doing. They didn't give a damn about what I said. I was only a burden to them. I wish I had succeeded at suicide so I could take the burden off their shoulders. That's the way I felt. And I really wished it had worked. But I also thought, 'I'm not killing myself instantly. I'm killing myself slowly.' I didn't want to do that.

"I decided that if I really was a pain in the ass to them [parents], I'd work for myself. And everything picked up after that. I started working at everything. My grades picked up, my appearance picked up. I dropped about sixty-five pounds. Everything just changed then."

The notion that death is final is not obvious to all teens. Adults may have difficulty remembering a time when they did not understand this. Some teens try suicide without understanding that death is permanent.

Robert, nineteen, told me about his suicide attempts. I asked him if the first couple of times he tried suicide, he thought death was final.

"Not really. I thought I'd just go somewhere else. What I did next [the first time he OD'd], I threatened to slash my wrists. I was trying everything.

And then it gets even better because I figured no one was taking me seriously, I couldn't do anything, so I got into stunt training. I figured if I died there I was getting paid for it and it wouldn't matter if I died there. I had no one else to worry about. It was a different type of suicide. I was by myself. I lived on the edges of buildings. It's scary because it's a long way down. But it doesn't really bother you because you figure, 'Well, okay, if I die, well, it's my time. It's one way of getting out of this thing [life].'

"Doing the stunts, well, it didn't bother me, but it bothered my friends. It scared them to death that I was so casual about it. I did it for kicks then. Walk on the edge of a building, on the outside of a bridge. It was a game with me then, flirting with death. When we did a stunt off a building we were supposed to have a wire holding us. I didn't use a wire. It was scary. I remember one time I wasn't really thinking about it and I almost slipped showing somebody something. And I remember how scared I was. It kind of snapped my mind out of it.

"It wasn't that I decided death was final right then. It was more getting all my act together. There was no need to die now. I could live my own life now. It really doesn't bother me now what other people do. I can make it on my own. I think it's a phase that people go through. That eventually, if they come close to death without actually dying, especially when they aren't meaning to die, and they know it, they'll snap out of it, teasing death like that. Life only matters if you're leaving someone behind. If you don't have anything, dying doesn't really matter too much." Yet Robert had decided that life was good now and he wanted me to tell other teens to hold onto it.

Tanya talked about trying to die and wanting to die and then suddenly talked about truly *not* wanting to die. That seems like a contradiction, but many said that they wanted to die at the same time they wanted to live. I asked her why she thought suicide was the only thing that would work for her.

"Because there was no one for me. And if there wasn't anybody then I couldn't live here all by myself. I didn't want to run away because I didn't want to hurt my parents because they'd never done anything to me." Yet Tanya had told me of parents who were cool to the point of indifference, who had high expectations of her, and of a father who abused her mother. Her life had not been happy. I asked if she thought suicide would hurt her parents.

"I wasn't planning to die."

Mike, my friend in Toronto with the punk haircut and the great sense of humour, told me about his suicide attempt.

"I took an overdose of sleeping pills. I was babysitting my sister's kid. The kid, who was two, was in bed. I took the pills and felt relief. I was hoping that it would finally be over. That's the way I wanted to go. Just fall asleep. I'd wanted to do it for so long and then I finally did it. I had thought about killing myself for about a year and a half.

"Every time I had a fight with my parents I'd think about suicide. Or if something bad happened at school, I'd be lying in my bedroom listening to music and I'd think about it.

"My sister came home early. She rushed me to the hospital and they made me throw up. But I didn't throw it all up so they pumped my stomach. It's gross. Thankfully, my parents didn't ever know about his. My sister kept her mouth shut. Like, I asked her not to tell. My sister and I are very close. We have no secrets from each other. I made a deal with her that I wouldn't try it again if she didn't tell our parents.

"The hospital psychiatrist saw me one day. He came in and talked about it, but I never saw him again. He didn't do anything. He didn't help me with my suicidal tendencies.

"I had thought about all the reasons why I needed to kill myself. I'd thought them all out in my head. I thought I had to do it because of all the things that were going on. I just didn't think anything was going to get better. It was either that or leave home and that didn't seem like it would help. It would just cause more problems."

I asked why running away wasn't an option.

"It would just cause new problems. You'd have to get a place to stay and all that.

"Just before I tried suicide, my girlfriend's father and little brother were killed in a car accident. Her whole family leaned on me. Her mother and brother. I was seventeen. My girlfriend had been telling her mother that she and I were going to get married in May, so her mother thought we were engaged and that explained why she leaned on me. She thought it was appropriate. I was out of town at my sister's when this happened and I flew to Toronto at six in the morning, the first flight. I stayed with my girlfriend for a while at the hospital. The thing that really worried me is that I'd never seen a dead body before, right? But I went to the wake and I saw them, both of them, the father and the child, lying there. And I couldn't cry. I didn't have any kind of inclination whatsoever to cry and that really worried me. It was so sad. I loved them both so much, especially the child. He was two years old. His second birthday was just two weeks past. He was such a sweetheart."

I asked, "Your girlfriend's abortion was first, so that this was like three deaths?"

"Exactly. My girlfriend was leaning on me a lot because her parents had just got separated." Mike looked up suddenly. "This sounds like a soap opera."

I asked if there was anything else.

"Probably. I went back to my sister's and the day I tried suicide I put the baby to bed at eight and then I took the pills and after I did it I was talking to a friend on the phone. He might have called my sister. He might have known I had taken something. Maybe that's why she came home early. It was the week after that had happened to my girlfriend's father and brother. It was really my first chance to be alone and to try something. When I had been home with my parents I had thought I didn't really want to go that way. I had another way I preferred. You know, I'd planned it out. Get in the garage and turn the car on. That way you just fall sleep. It's a lot easier and less painful. But my sister didn't have a garage so I had to go with my second choice. Pills.

"When I tried suicide, yeah, I thought death was final. I don't believe in life after death. I just thought it would be better to die. I didn't expect to survive. I hoped not to.

"Somebody should have listened to me and maybe just talked to me like a good friend or something. Helped me out."

Whenever teens told me about why they tried suicide, it seemed that whatever happened leading to the decision – whether a long, drawn-out deliberation over the course of weeks, or a quick, impulsive one made in minutes – came as a result of months, sometimes years of problems at home. Of course, that may not be true for all. Some may truly have a sudden, compelling yearning to take their own life.

Janet told me, "I stole some money at school when I was twelve. I got suspended. My grandmother said, 'Don't think about running away because the police will catch you.' I didn't want to go through what I was going to have to go through with the principal and everything so I just took some pills. And nothing happened. I thought they were strong. I threw up quite a bit. But nothing happened. I don't think anyone knew. I told my girlfriend a long time after."

Janet tried suicide again at seventeen. I asked her why suicide was an option.

"I wouldn't be here to face life, right? I'd be gone. I wouldn't have to cope. I thought of death as just not being here."

I asked her what she hoped would happen when she tried suicide.

"I wish I'd have died." Four of the teens answered this question that way. But when I asked Janet what would change her mind if she was thinking of suicide right now, she said, "Just a little light at the end of the tunnel. Even a little light."

If she thought that life would get better, if she had some hope, then she would try to cope.

## EMOTIONS

Emotional turmoil seems to be the normal state of teen life. Many of us remember these years as being very stressful and difficult. Changing hormones, physical characteristics, lack of experience in social and sexual roles, pressures of career and school choices, changing friendships outside the home, and evolving family dynamics within the home all contribute to the emotional stresses on teens.

Teens often have not yet developed a vocabulary to describe their emotions and so find them difficult to talk about. They feel "bad" or "depressed," but they can't describe their feelings in detail. They may not know a trusted adult to confide in, and they may not even be aware what they are feeling. Their emotions prior to attempting suicide may not be obvious to them. Suzanne, the young woman who talked to me in her home in Calgary, described her feelings when I asked her how she felt before she tried suicide.

"Before? You know when you're going to cry and you get a lump in your throat? Well, it's just like the lump is your whole body. You're always tense inside and you don't trust yourself."

I asked her how long she had felt like that.

"It's hard to say the first time because I'd never had much happiness before that with my family. It was at least a month, but I'd never been really happy, so maybe it was years."

All the teens I spoke to had suffered losses, as everyone has losses in life. It's normal. But it seemed that the teens I interviewed did not know how to react to those losses, or even recognize that they are part of life. They reacted to their losses – whether it was the break-up with a girlfriend or boyfriend, a grade lower than they expected, the death of a pet, or a move away from friends – with an all-body despair that plunged them into hopelessness. It is hard for anyone else to gauge the degree of reaction, and teens very often don't understand it themselves.

While most teens react quickly to emotional pain, some see themselves as extremely sensitive. It is possible that these teens suffer from low self-esteem and thus accept blame and negative comments more readily than those with self-confidence. But some do seem to be more attuned to their emotions than others, picking up feelings and intuitively understanding them without reasoning. Such sensitivity is not "bad" in itself. Psychologists, psychiatrists, nurses, social workers, doctors, veterinarians, teachers, musicians, actors, and writers often possess this sensitivity. It may be their strength: they are more compassionate and understanding of others. Such sensitivity can make a teen more vulnerable to rejection and criticism, and more likely to try to escape the emotional pain via suicide.

The emotions that went with their suicidal actions were many and varied, but they seemed to stem from their reaction to loss, their feelings of rejection by family and friends, and low self-esteem. When these feelings got more than they could bear, they began to plan to kill themselves. They felt bewildered by their pain and didn't see any future, so they stopped making plans.

# THREE

# Coping Strategies
# and Change

*I am resting and waiting, waiting*
*for an answer to an unknown*
*question, it will come.*
*But leave me alone*
*don't touch the walls I have so*
*carefully built, don't penetrate the*
*isolation which I have retreated into,*
*for now it is safe to think. . . .*

– B.B.

Humans are amazing in their ability to cope with very difficult situations, but some teens, given certain circumstances, may respond to such situations – stress, depression, hopelessness, feelings of despair – with antisocial behaviour. Reckless driving, drug and alcohol abuse, constant TV-watching, and other socially isolating activities help some teens to cope with their emotions and allow them to manage. Some feel such emotional pain and see so few methods of escape that when they do find a coping mechanism that helps, they desperately repeat it, even if it is unhealthy or even illegal.

## CONTROLLING LIFE

The teens I interviewed told me that at some point in their life, whether for a few weeks or a few months or years, life became too difficult; problem piled on top of problem, and there seemed no way of solving any of them. They floundered in an ocean of troubles and felt there was no direction for them but down. Surviving became a series of controlling strategies, ways of keeping their worst feelings from overwhelming them.

69

They tried to deal with such problems, and often managed for long periods by controlling themselves if they could not control those around them. Some exhibited obsessive-compulsive behaviours, such as always keeping their keys, clothes, and books in designated places, washing their hands thirty times a day, or eating foods only in a certain order. In a sense, such behaviours are bids for personal safety. If the strategies they use to keep themselves from being overcome by pain are successful, even if only temporarily, then they will continue to use them. Often without being able to name their pain, the teens I interviewed exhibited behaviours that seemed to alleviate their feelings of despair, such as over-eating.

They looked for a respite, a time of peace, a place to hide. Sometimes they hid themselves in rigid behaviours, sometimes in a change of appearance. Adopting a particular look gave them some control over the way people responded to them. They would dress in a way that made others, including their parents, believe they were a certain kind of person – someone with no ambition, for instance. The teens hid behind such façades as they tried to deal with their problems and successfully diverted their parents' attention from themselves to their appearance, a subject they could handle, and away from what they were feeling.

ESCAPING PAIN

If the teens could not control their pain, they had strategies that allowed them to escape it. For many of us, escape in the form of "being absent" from the present is often used to deal with difficult days. We may "veg out" on Friday night in front of the television to escape the travails of the week, or go to the pub on Saturday night with friends, or take off on a Sunday afternoon picnic. We watch television, read books, drink, listen to music, or go to a movie so that we can occupy our minds and our emotions without having to deal with the problems we face in real life. Everyone does some or all of these things throughout their lives. Problems arise, however, when the amount of time we spend escaping is excessive. Some teens told me that just before their suicide attempt they daydreamed all the time. They seemed to live in a world of fantasy and seldom paid attention to what was going on around them. Some told me they would go to school, then come home and spend all their time alone in their bedrooms, listening to music for hours on end. They would do anything to keep themselves from thinking or feeling too much.

Sometimes these ways of coping help a great deal by releasing emotional pressure, but teens who are suicidal use escape much of the time. It may be as simple as daydreaming for hours, or as dangerous as using psychoactive drugs which change one's thoughts, ideas, and behaviour. Teens may get temporary relief from their problems, but by doing so they avoid dealing with their need for love, attention, and acceptance. The teens I interviewed knew escape didn't work because it didn't ultimately rid them of their emotional pain.

Often the teens tried to deal with their ever-increasing problems by escaping into booze and drugs. Bruce said, "I'd been feeling bad for years before the suicide attempt. I was drinking and getting high and I was thinking, 'Hey. This isn't me. I should be better.' I couldn't get it [the schoolwork] in school. I felt like I was dumb. I felt like an outcast. I felt like Linus with the blanket. Everybody talks to him, but nobody likes him. They see him walking down the street, they go, 'Hi, Linus,' and keep walking. That's how I felt."

Janet lived with her grandparents who were like a mother and father to her. She couldn't talk to them. The problems at home and school got so unmanageable that at the age of fourteen she started to drink. Within two years she was drinking most of the time.

"I was scared of the future. I don't know, people say we're heading for another depression, and I don't want to live through that."

I asked her what it felt like to be drunk every day.

"I was really hurting. I was a basket case. I'd go to school and I'd be shaking like a leaf, right? My relationship with my grandparents was zero in those days. My grades were bad, but they'd never been good. I told my grandparents my grades were my problem and I'd get what I wanted. They said, 'Well, we love you so much. We don't want to see your life fucked up,' and all this stuff. 'Well, it's my life. I'll do what I want. Get pregnant. Go on welfare.' They said, 'We don't want to hear you talking like this.' But they were never really straight with me.

"Up to the time I was eighteen my life was just hell. I didn't like it. I didn't really have many friends. I don't know, I just wasn't happy. I suffered a lot emotionally. I had really little self-esteem, really little self-respect. I didn't think anybody liked me. I was picked on a lot."

I asked her why she thought that was.

"I don't know. Maybe because I was fat or something. I think that was the main one. I went to school every day anticipating a rotten day. I didn't want to go. I was drinking all the time then.

"I can't think of anything that could have helped me then. My grandparents and I never had a listening relationship. I was always put out of the way. When I was younger they were really close to me. I can remember my grandfather playing ball with me and everything. But that was it."

I observed that when I talked, she listened intently. I asked her how she learned to listen.

Janet laughed with surprise and a little embarrassment. "Going to AA meetings."

Not all the teens I interviewed used alcohol or drugs as an escape before they tried suicide. Some suffered quiet anguish, withdrew, isolated themselves physically from family and friends, and then tried to die.

### DENIAL

Denial is another strategy that most people use to some extent in their daily lives. We tell ourselves that our job isn't that bad, that our relationship with our parents is okay, or that difficulties with our partner will ease over time. We use denial to cope with everyday problems.

Some teens who had tried to die by suicide dealt with their overwhelming problems by denying much of their existence. They lived every day as if their growing emotional difficulties simply didn't exist, and that the increasing practical dilemmas – school grades, jobs, a place to stay – didn't matter.

Beth told me that she hadn't realized that she was in so much denial until she went to a psychiatrist and got help understanding what was going on in her life. "I really had a neat trick. I just didn't think about it [her problems]. When something happened to me I'd just store it away. . . . Then, later, it was like a dam had burst and I had all these things piled up.

"I know the problems are there but I just looked at them through a window or something, not really look at them. . . . I don't let the full impact of them hit me. I don't think about why a thing happens or what I'm going to do about it. I just store it away.

"Then, unfortunately, it all comes out at once and I get depressed. So I've tried to start working on things now as they happen. A lot of things with my family are still hidden away. They're there. I can sit here and talk about them as if they had happened to another person. I don't get into crying fits. But a lot of this came out afterwards and it was like, 'Oh, yeah. I remember this and I remember that.' All these different pieces of the story finally fall together."

It seemed to many of the teens I interviewed that their parents were strong, that they seemed to manage *their* lives without great emotional upheaval, and were able to deal with problems without getting upset. In this scenario, denial looks like an effective strategy. Few got any help in learning how to handle their feelings.

Denial is also combined with wishful thinking. Teens would like their relationship with their parents to be good, so they convince themselves that the relationship is indeed good – in spite of what reality tells them.

Beth did not accept that her parents didn't love her, or that her parents' "love" was not helpful to her. Although she told me she was abused as a child, she did not equate that with not being loved.

"I've been living away from home for fifteen months now. I had no self-esteem when I first left. But Jim [her boyfriend], in the last few months, has been trying to convince me that I'm pretty."

With her auburn curls, green eyes, and creamy skin, she was stunning and I told her so.

"Oh no. I was raised with, 'You have to lose weight, Beth. You're not pretty. You're not this.'

"If someone said, 'Gee, you look nice,' I'd think, 'No, I don't. You're just saying that to make me feel good.' Like I honestly thought I was really, really ugly. So now I'm at the point where I think I don't look half-bad. Sure I knew I was intelligent, but at the same time they'd [her parents] said I was lazy. And my personality. . . . They said I was bitchy, I cried too much, or, 'You're too fat, Beth. Your hair looks like a rat's nest,' or, 'You don't dress right.' I never did anything right. I grew up with it."

Beth was often hit when she was young. Her dad beat her with a belt. At sixteen she hit him back.

"I felt bad. I'd never do it again."

I questioned that *she* felt bad.

"Well, of course. This is my father. I should respect him."

I asked her if she respected people who hit women.

"My father never laid a hand on my mother.

"I think it was because I was his daughter. It's funny we should talk about this, because when I was in the psychiatric ward I heard some awful stories. One girl, her father used to sexually molest her. One, her teacher did and no one believed her. Another, her father used to chase her around with a hatchet."

I asked if her dad sexually molested her.

"I don't know. I've been told. My mother used to hint at things when I was younger, but I don't remember. Nothing when I was a teenager."

So Beth thought that in spite of the treatment she received from her parents, her parents were good, and she was bad.

## RESISTANCE

Some of the teens responded to their problems with a strategy of resistance. They objected loudly and often dramatically to parental authority with the goal of getting at least some reaction from and emotional involvement with their parents. They hit back physically when parents hit them, and responded to arguments with parents or siblings with sarcasm, yelling, and loud music. Resistance takes the form of behaving in ways the teens know their parents hate in order to get their attention – getting poor grades, coming home drunk, leaving condoms around where parents would see them, shoplifting and getting caught, or wearing clothes they think parents would find offensive. Resistance is a strategy parents are accustomed to from very young children, but some teens continue to use this pattern of dealing with problems because it demands a reaction. The reaction might not be positive, but to the teen any reaction is better than indifference or denial.

## RESILIENCE

Studies indicate that there are certain characteristics in individuals which make suicide less likely.[1] Having a sense of humour helps. Perhaps it reminds teens that there is more than one way to look at a problem and creates the kind of broad thinking needed to find other options. A history of creative problem-solving helps as well. Those who are successful at problem-solving will be less likely to be overwhelmed by any feelings of helplessness. These are characteristics that one would expect to find in an optimistic person, and it may be they are the result of that optimism, not the cause of it.

Personal characteristics of optimism, autonomy, and humour may protect teens from suicide. Family relationships that include loving and attentive parents, and no family history of suicide, also help. Teens who are pro-active in life, who feel in charge of of their own destiny, enjoy a sense of personal autonomy. This, combined with an attentive and accepting group of friends, and a culture that accepts and supports teens in time of trouble or harassment, letting them know that they are important and necessary, gives teens a sense of resilience against any problems that may arise.

Teens come to this resilience through experience with people and problems. Such experience may encourage them to view problems as a "learning experience," rather than something insurountable. Resilience comes from a history of successes in life; feelings of helplessness arise from a legacy of failures where problems are ignored, set aside, trivialized, or solved by others.

Teens need to be shown how to deal with problems. They need to be shown what's expected of them, where they fit into their families and into their social group. They need to accept their mistakes as a way of learning and not as evidence of basic incompetence or wickedness. Being allowed to fail is a way of learning. When a child is five, his parents teach him how to tie his shoes; they don't turn him over to social welfare because he couldn't tie a knot the first time he tried. Yet, when the same boy turns thirteen, some parents seem to think he should suddenly know how to act in any and all situations. In some families of the teens I interviewed, no one took the time to help them recognize the fact they were going to make mistakes in their lives. How could they avoid mistakes unless they spent all day in their rooms avoiding life altogether?

Most of the teens didn't want to leave their parents and strike out on their own, making one mistake after another. They just wanted the freedom to try things their way and then come back home and talk about it, figure things out, then go out and try life again. They wanted a home base, a support system, and acceptance of who they were, mistakes and all.

## DEALING WITH PAIN

Many teens found it impossible to deal with their emotional pain. They knew that other teens dealt successfully with feelings of loneliness, rejection, and isolation from their families, and they didn't understand why they couldn't. They felt different, and less capable. Many had been taught by their parents that they didn't have to deal with pain. When they had scraped their knee and it hurt, parents put a bandage on it. When they had a headache, parents gave them an aspirin. The principle of pain tolerance in most families was that if you had pain, someone would fix it; you weren't supposed to endure it. No one sat down with the teens when they were children and told them that pain was part of living, that everyone has to deal with some pain, both physical and emotional, on some level, and that there are effective ways of doing it. They needed a parent or a mentor to teach them that they could deal with their emotional pain by crying, writing, or talking about it. But no one did. So teens tried to see what other people did; they looked for cues from their parents.

Janet watched how her grandparents coped. "My grandmother would go into her bedroom and cry. That's how she dealt with it. My grandfather would yell so loud the whole house would shake. When I was a kid I was scared of him, but as I got older I thought, 'I can stand up to him.' And so we'd get to the point where we'd just be glaring at each other. Nobody knew who was going to make the first move and my grandmother would just be standing there like we were TNT going to go off any second." That angry reaction didn't help Janet cope with her emotional stress.

Robert's parents used denial. "They used to walk away. They'd argue and then say, 'I don't want to hear another word.' That's it. I was supposed to stop thinking. Just like that. Even though the emotions would be very intense. I think what hurt everyone more than anything else was just to stop and let everything stay at that level. They'd say, 'Don't say it. I don't want to hear another word about it.' That always got me. They'd say, 'Shut up.' And I'd say 'No.' And that would get them more angry with me."

Teresa also watched her parents handle emotions with denial. They pretended there were no problems. She was having a lot of trouble but her parents dismissed it as unimportant. "The problems were a combination of things. Parents were probably the major thing. Friends were pressuring me to do things I didn't really want to do and I got suckered into doing a lot of things I didn't really want to do. And I felt like shit for doing them. But the pressures I got were unbelievable and my parents seemed to shrug that off.

"I hated myself for doing what other people told me to do just because they said so. That's another thing my parents used all the time. 'Do this because we said so. What you want doesn't matter. You have to do it our way.'"

Teresa decided to do it her way.

"I remember sitting there and methodically taking an Anacin and a sip of Coke and then another Anacin and then another sip of Coke. I sat there and watched myself get sick. It was bizarre. I sat on the chair and watched myself in the mirror as my body started to get sick. I had a sort of perverse sense of satisfaction. I thought, 'Actually, this might do it.' For about four or five months afterwards I had uncontrollable shaking. My nerves were shot.

"I was totally a nervous wreck. That was the last time I tried it [suicide] and I thought, I'm not doing anything this way. I'm not accomplishing anything."

I asked her if she wanted to suffer, or if she wanted her parents to see her suffer.

"Yeah. I wanted them to watch this, but they weren't there. They were upstairs, sound asleep. I tried to make some noise. To maybe get them down there so they could see what was happening. But it didn't wake them up. I made a lot of noise without having them come and yell at me. They finally came down the next morning. I was supposed to be up already for school and my mom came in and said, 'How come you're not up?' And there was this bucket beside the bed and I had been throwing up all night. All over everything. I tried not to, but my body kept throwing things up.

"I was drained. And she said, 'What's the matter? Aren't you feeling good?' I didn't say anything. This had whacked out my hearing a bit, too. It sounded as though she was standing about six feet away, or six miles away. I could hear her, just faintly, and I looked up and said, 'Mom?' and I couldn't see. I couldn't hear right. 'Mom, are you there?'

"She said, 'What the hell are you doing? You're supposed to be up for school already. Get going.'

"She looked around and saw the Anacin bottle on the dresser and the bottle of Coke spilled all over the carpet and she said, 'You got a headache?'

"I said, 'Mom, I've got a hell of a lot more than a headache,' and I just laid back down.

"She said, 'What did you do?'

"I wasn't about to tell her I tried to kill myself. I just lay there. She started yelling and screaming and calling me a stupid kid and what was I trying to prove?

"I just gave up trying to talk to her and rolled over and said, 'Leave me alone. Get the hell out of here.' I tried to go to sleep. Then my dad came in. Like Mom must have gone upstairs and said, 'Come here, John. Look at this one.'

"He came in and said 'God! Kids!' and he walked out.

"And I lay there and cried and cried. And they never came in again and they never said anything. It didn't do a damn thing. It didn't matter what I did." Teresa's parents denied her problems existed even when they could *see* the problem. They pretended that nothing was seriously wrong.

Jake had a good relationship with his father, but his parents were divorced and living separately. He learned different ways of dealing with emotions.

"My mom yells, and she doesn't stop. I yell back. I don't like being yelled at. Like I could understand if she yelled at me once, but she goes on and on. She doesn't stop when I yell back, but I can't just sit there and let her treat me like that. Sometimes I just take off, leave the house. But when I come back it's even worse, like, 'How dare you leave?' And that kind of thing. I prefer it better just to get, out.

"When my dad gets angry, he won't yell at you. He'll still do things for you. My mom just yells and won't do anything. I like to get away from my mom when she's mad. Talking to her doesn't work. But with other people . . . I, like . . . talk to them, work it out verbally. I say, 'Hey, you did this and I don't like it,' and kind of rationalize. It works better."

COPING WITH EMOTIONS

Most of the teens I interviewed learned from their families and from experience to think of emotions as "bad." Anger, fear, and sadness are to be feared, suppressed, and denied. Suzanne found that she wasn't supposed to be anything but happy. "If you're in a family it's always that you have to be so happy! My mom always demands [happiness]. If I'm really depressed and I'm walking around the house sad, she says, 'What's wrong with you? Why are you being such a bitch?' It's like I want to say, 'Leave me alone.'

But we're supposed to make her happy. We have to. She has to stop and make us happy. No one's allowed to be unhappy around her. I knew I was in trouble with my parents when my attitude was mopey, so I have to cover up those feelings. I always felt that. I couldn't be unhappy, I couldn't be hurt. I couldn't be sad. And you feel everyone else is like that, hiding things."

Suzanne saw emotions as risky. "I don't show my mother my emotions. I either tell them to Tanya [her girlfriend] or call my brother, or cry and think for a while. And once I get myself together I can tell my mom about it. She can tell when I'm sad or whatever, but I've got control over it."

I asked her if it would be it be disastrous for her to lose control in front of her mother or dad.

"Yeah."

I wanted to know why.

"Then I'd have to depend on them. I couldn't depend on them before. I always had to depend on myself. So I wouldn't really know how they would take it. I'm afraid of my temper. I kind of have to hold it down and it's bottled. Sometimes I have to be alone to let it explode, right? Disperse, sort of. I think emotions aren't socially acceptable.

"Even if you're too happy, it's not acceptable. Then everyone thinks you're spinny. If you're going out somewhere, and you're waiting at the bus stop and you're dancing around, people are watching you. And you feel so. . . . You think, 'What am I doing? I know I'm acting weird, but this is the way I feel.' That's not socially acceptable."

I asked if she thought being happy was suspect.

"Yeah. You're a teenager. If you're happy, you must be on drugs."

So many teens were afraid to risk showing their emotions to their parents. Often, they had good reason for being afraid, because their parents ridiculed them, used what the teen told them against him or her at another time, or told their friends and thus betrayed the teens' confidence. Teens who experienced this no longer felt they could trust their parents and no longer felt they could confide in them. But the teens still needed help with their feelings, and because they couldn't talk to their parents and didn't know where else to go, they felt helpless. They usually wanted help, but didn't understand how important it was to get it.

Many teens told me that, more than anything else, they needed to be accepted before they could change their behaviour. Otherwise it wasn't safe to change.

Suzanne said, "My parents put a lot of pressure on me, always nagging, about my attitude, my personality, character. It was everything. They didn't like the way I was acting. I was going out too much. Everything I was doing was wrong. And maybe it was. But they should have told me in a different way. When school started again there was a lot of pressure from there. The teachers put pressure on me to do better in school and to change my attitude, and my parents were fighting all the time and I needed attention. I needed some kind of different attention than what I was getting.

"I was popular. My friends were okay. But they didn't really know me. At that age, it's so important to be like everyone else that you don't really find out who you are. I didn't know who I was. I didn't know what I wanted. It was really tough."

Suzanne told me what many others said, that everything seemed to be too much and they couldn't decide what it was they should do and what would make life better, so they reacted to the pressure in ways that they hoped would resolve their problems. They tried to control their world and themselves by rigidly conforming. They tried harder to be the perfect child, with perfect grades and perfect clothes. They returned home from dates on time, cleaned their rooms, and always had a smile on their face. But beneath the surface they tried escape, withdrawing to their rooms, and to the crowd of kids they hung around with, to music, to alcohol and drugs. They tried denial, pretending all was well, that the drugs and alcohol were really only occasional that their compounding problems were really not so bad. They tried resistance. Life became confusing and painful.

## REJECTION

Some teens lived in an environment where they were ridiculed and belittled and where no one showed them how to cope, or expected that they would cope well. After they reached about thirteen, they started to see how their family interacted in patterned and typical behviours; they began to understand that they were rejected. Up to this point they had tried to pretend to themselves that deep down their parents truly loved them. After thirteen they were more realistic, perhaps more capable of coping with the knowledge that their parents' meager love was not enough, or that while their parents loved them in their fashion, they were inept as parents, or too overwhelmed by their own problems to help their children. Parents may have loved their teens, but were so emotionally upset with each other that they had no energy to deal with the teens' problems. In some cases, parents simply did not love their child.

As the children grew into teens, they started to see how their parents used them. They did not want to be used as a bouncing ball between them, as a scapegoat for all the blame in the family, or as a focus for fights, so they turned away and that caused changes in the family; it caused friction. When teens got older they started to create a power base of their own, which often did not fit with their family's view of itself.


MAKING CHANGES

*I have no hands*
> *yet my life is in my hands*

– B.B.


The multiple problems in the teens' lives that pushed them to consider suicide caused an overwhelming emotional pain that made everything but the pain itself seem unimportant. Such pain is hard for others to understand. I tried to equate it to my past experience and remember at fifteen suffering severe physical pain from a broken hip. The pain was so bad, so overwhelming, that I would have done anything to get away from it; I wanted morphine (and got it) so I could escape into blackness. The emotional pain preceding suicide must be like that. Escape is crucial, even if it means trying to take your own life.

But pain doesn't stay at the same level for anyone. When teens didn't complete suicide and life went on, their pain level changed, but seldom did the source of their problems. No magic fairy godmother transformed their parents into loving, caring people if they were the source of the problem; there was no emotional antidote. Most often the change that made life easier, more possible, came from within. Their change in attitude was the strongest, most permanent change I saw.

The change in attitude toward themselves was often dramatic; they suddenly understood something important about themselves. For some, this was the understanding that nothing in their family was going to change; they were alone; they would get no help at home. Along with this revelation came the idea that they were valuable in spite of their parents' negative assessment, and that even though they had choosen suicide as their means of escape, it wasn't inevitable. A revelation such as this made a great difference in their attitude, and they found that they now viewed life quite differently. They realized they had more control over life, more opportunities, more future, and that control was not in the outside world, but in themselves.

In other cases, changes in teens' lives came from external circumstances: an abusive parent left; parents became more understanding; a counsellor who helped. These changes made enough difference in their lives that slowly they made other changes for themselves. After a while, they realized that they were able to cope with life. Slowly, they groped their way out of the fog, step by step, finding a path that was leading them to a more positive life. They weren't sure they were going to succeed, but when they looked back at how far they had come, they realized they had gained some level of self-confidence.

"My parents love me," I heard teens say often. In their recovery, however, many of the teens were forced to re-examine their troubled relationships with their parents.

If teens felt that their parents really loved them and cared for them, but abused and neglected them because they, the teens, were unloveable and basically "bad," then the teens were co-operating in their own destruction. For some, this was preferable to admitting that they were not loved. In those circumstances it was very hard to break free of the attitude that they were "no good" and that they were helpless to change their own lives.

Leslie tried to make excuses for her mother, to find a reason why her mother couldn't help her. She did not want to think that her mother did not care.

"I wished she would have talked to me, but I always made excuses for her. 'Oh, she's too tired.' 'She's all grown up.' 'She's getting old.' 'She has to get up in the morning.' I made all these excuses for why she wouldn't talk to me."

Sometimes they couldn't see that there was anything wrong with their family; the peculiar patterns of abuse were so constant and so long-term that they began to seem normal. Teens thought all the problems lay within themselves, and that the family was fine.

I met Tanya at a park. We sat on a bench in the sunshine watching the ducks on the water and the children playing on the grass. Tanya was intelligent and insightful when she talked about her life. She saw her parents as loving providers who were trying hard to help her.

82

"I get constant praise now, after all this [suicide attempts]. And that's pressure in itself. Actually that's the way it's always been. I've always been sort of put upon a pedestal. And they always say to my sister, 'Why can't you be like Tanya? She's so good.' And that's bad for her and it's bad for me. And that means I can never make a mistake. And when I feel myself making mistakes I stop and I pull back and I say to myself, 'What would Dad want?' So that's what I do a lot. The little girl syndrome. Try to please everybody else. If you happen to please yourself by doing that, then that's a bonus.

"My father never tells me what to do. I mean, I make my own choices. Whatever I do he always says it's good enough for him. But I feel like it's not.

"I have this vision of my dad as being this god-like perfect kind of man who can impress anyone in the world, who makes millions of dollars a year, and I can never achieve any of that. And that's where I feel inadequate. Totally inadequate.

"I feel like I hold my family together. See, my parents don't get along very well. As far back as I can remember I've been their mediator. I can remember when I was four or five years old and every time they fought it would be me jumping in the middle saying, 'Please don't fight, please don't fight.' They'd get mad and my dad would grab me by the arm and take me out. He'd leave and I'd go with him. I didn't want to go with him. I wanted to be with my mom. I hated him. He scared me. So I always feel that I have to keep it together. My sister's a basket case. She doesn't know what she wants to do. She just wants to lounge around for the rest of her life. My parents are sort of up in arms about that. I know she feels that I get all the attention. And it's true. I do. I get all the attention, which I don't really need.

"Not for a minute do I blame my parents. And I will never blame my parents. You know, I'm just a victim of circumstance."

Tanya blames herself for her feelings of inadequacy, yet she tells me that she had had tremendous pressures placed on her to achieve, to be the perfect child, to be the one who held the family together. She doesn't feel valued for who she is, only for what she can do.

I asked the teens I interviewed what they thought had to change before suicide was no longer an option.

Mike and Jake told me that suicide was always an option. Strictly speaking, that's true. The possibility of taking one's own life is there for everyone. But most teens interpreted the question to mean, when is suicide no longer something they really wanted to do?

Suzanne said, "I needed to know that somebody was there for me. Maybe I needed my parents. Like, I know that if I went to my mom and said, 'Hey, Mom, I'm considering suicide, will you help me?' She'd say, 'What? Why? It's so stupid.' I'd just kind of slink out of the room. So the rules have to change to, 'Don't put me down. Don't tell me I'm wrong. Just help me.'"

Someone did talk to Leslie after her suicide attempt, which made a huge difference in her life. Two friends spent hours talking to her, which helped her over the very worst of her depression and sustained her through the months that followed. Once Leslie had confidence in herself she was able to improve her relationship with her mother.

Sometimes the teens made a physical change; they left home, because they knew their family patterns were destructive and they could see no way of changing those patterns while still living in that environment.

It is possible to stay at home and get love and attention from non-family members. Teens need strong friendships, need to feel accepted by their peers. A caring friend may also help them to make small, important changes in their relationships with their family. Some teens may find it difficult to talk to anyone in their family, but they can try other ways of reaching them besides direct conversation. They can record a message on a tape deck, or leave a letter to be read; they can ask a school counsellor, social worker, or other professional to come home to talk to their parents with them. Even if the family reacts negatively to such attempts at better communication, the teen is better off for having tried to improve their family relationships.

But teens must recognize that their problems are not the result of failures in themselves. It is only through such insight that they can move past their problems to a happier life. Janet does it with the Alcoholics Anonymous motto: "One day at a time."

I was overcome by the bravery and honesty of the teens I interviewed. I found it difficult to conduct more than two interviews a day because of the emotional impact. I understood the courage it took for them to keep on living after having endured such pain and had to deal with my anger that, so often, they should be so alone. These teens weren't expecting anything from me; they knew that I was collecting information for a book and was not a therapist, so they weren't looking for information or help – they only wanted to tell their own stories.

And while I was sometimes upset at what they had to deal with, I found that the most difficult thing to bear was the conviction of those who felt they deserved all the troubles they had. I was furious with their parents, with their teachers, with myself, with all of society for allowing any child to grow up feeling like that. The positive aspect of this assessment is that such teens felt change was their own responsibility. If they wanted life to be different, they knew they would have to be the ones to make it so.

## HOW TEENS CAN HELP THEMSELVES

*I would hold your hand in the stormy skies*
*I would cradle your head in a hurricane of madness*
*I would wipe your brow and face the fire*
*and I would not relent, I would not relent.*

– B.B.

When the teens were in pain – when suicide appeared as the only escape route – they often did not have the energy nor the ability to make big corrective changes in their lives; they were not able to clearly see what they needed. If a white knight had arrived on a horse and invited them to ride off with him, they would have escaped with him in a flash, but white knights were in short supply and, as so many of them accurately saw, they were usually alone to deal with their problems themselves. Nothing in the real world looked worthwhile. When they were in pain, every path looked too hard to take, every option too difficult to try. If they had advice to give at that time it would have been: don't try to make grand changes, but small ones, until the pain begins to subside.

It may be difficult to move from being withdrawn and silent to being open and forthcoming about one's problems, but the first step might be to seek out someone to talk to. Most couldn't talk to their parents, but some did have a favourite relative. Suzanne sometimes talked to her brother and Mike to his sister. Anna talked to her teacher, but only briefly and not intimately. According to most, there doesn't seem to be enough time in school schedules to develop the kind of relationship with a teacher that would make it possible to confide in him or her.

Suicide remains a taboo subject, one of those social unmentionables that is not discussed very often. Some of the teens felt even talking about suicide was "wrong," a shameful idea, and didn't want to admit even to thinking about it. They thought that anyone they confided in would either tell them they were crazy or that they were wrong to think about it rather than try to understand their feelings. If they did feel they could talk to someone about it, it was usually a friend.

But picking the right friend can be tricky. Two of the teens I interviewed told me that they had talked to people who were also suicidal and that they had no energy to help. They needed to talk to someone who was sensible and "together," and who would take them seriously. But some people feel uncomfortable talking about suicide and don't want to hear about it. They aren't used to intimacy, may feel threatened by other people's revelations, and won't listen when a teen approaches for help.

It is often necessary for teens to have several friends to try talking to. If the friends won't listen, the teen needs to be prepared to feel rejected, foolish, and even more worthless than before. It may be difficult to try talking to someone else, but it is necessary. Finding a compassionate friend willing to listen may be the most important thing a troubled teen does, and they need to keep trying.

It is important for troubled teens to see positive change in the long-term relationship with their families, but they must realize that circumstances won't change instantly. There is no quick-fix solution, no sudden revelation in which their parents suddenly realize what a great person the teen is. Change in the relationship with parents takes time, perhaps years. It can help teens to set reasonable goals with their parents, or rather goals that concern their parents: two-week, two-month, two-year goals. The lines of communication need to be open: what kind of change do they want? What is possible?

As well as changing the ways of interacting with parents, teens often need to change the way they deal with stress. Some teens I interviewed had little practice in dealing with stress. Bodies can respond well to some techniques of relaxation and control, which are often taught in aerobics classes, gym classes at school, or meditation groups. These exercises may not relieve the overwhelming pain of a suicidal person, but they may help the day-to-day problems that become large ones if not dealt with properly.

Teens may need to change their environment. Some quit or changed schools, moved out of their house, into an apartment of their own, to another city, or onto the streets.

Diana was fifteen years old. She met me for coffee along with her boyfriend, who had also attempted suicide. Diana had been abandoned by her mother at the age of five and her grandmother at ten. At fourteen she started living in a park, where she stayed for several months, using her boyfriend's mother's house as a place to wash and change.

Sometimes this kind of change in the teens' lives relieved them of the constant criticism they received from their parents. Easing the pressure was enough to allow them to see themselves for who they were rather than what their parents told them. If they moved to an atmosphere where they were accepted on their own terms, then they seemed to be able to re-assess themselves, and even start to like themselves.

But some told me that they felt they had no place to go. They read the "Do not hitch-hike" signs, and watched movies about street kids and drugs and prostitution, and felt the world outside their houses, outside their social circle, looked dangerous. This observation worried me a lot. They were young; why didn't the world outside their families look like an adventure? Their low self-esteem might be responsible for this attitude that while others could "make it" out there in the world, they felt they could not.

There also seems to be a "cult of excellence" weighing teens down. Parents, teachers, television, and newspapers tell them that they must succeed, that they must be the very best − implicitly, not the very best they can be, but better than everyone else. This didn't seem to be an ambition when I was a teen. I knew perfectly well I wasn't the best in anything. Neither were my friends. We were expected to do well, but not necessarily to be the most accomplished in the community. Why aren't teens today allowed to take their time, be happy? Why this frantic rush to succeed? Of the teens I interviewed, most were afraid that they'd fail in life. They were already suffering from a loss of self-esteem and often didn't think they deserved a good life. It all looked overwhelming.

So what can teens do if they can't make the major change of leaving home? Find a friend to talk to. Try calling a crisis center, a distress center, a youth helpline − telephone numbers are listed prominently in phone books. If teens live in rural areas, they can call the operator and ask for help; operators will connect them with the nearest distress center. And if a teen talks to someone at a distress center and doesn't feel they are helping, they should try again at another time and talk to someone else. The idea is to keep trying, to not give up hope.

Teens can also find help on the Internet. There are, as every teen should know, predators online, so they need to pick a site that will be useful and safe. Sites like *SuicideInfo.ca* have links to sites for teenagers and depression, suicide prevention, and how to help friends in crisis, and *KidsHelp.sympatico.ca* has an "ask a counsellor" section. Not only can teens log onto the Internet and correspond with other teens, there are also sites such as the KidsHelp line which give them a chance to have their questions or concerns answered.

Community resources are often posted on bulletin boards at schools as well as being listed in the phone book. Community agencies are listed in the front of the phone book or under "Family Services" in the white pages. Family Services offices may recommend where to get counselling.

The process of getting help from community services, however, can be frustrating. It's not uncommon to get referred to several different people before getting the right person to talk to. When a receptionist answers the phone, it is better to say, "Can you tell me where I can get a counsellor for suicide prevention?" rather than, "I'm thinking of suicide." Receptionists want to hear questions they can answer. One day I tested this, calling the Family Service Center near me. I got an answering service. Someone phoned me back four hours later. I called the Mental Health Clinic where the phone rang twelve times before a receptionist answered. It was frustrating even though I was not in emotional distress; it would be a great deal more frustrating if the caller felt helpless to start with.

Sometimes when teens most need help, they don't have the energy it takes to ask for it. They feel so depressed and tired all the time that they can't pick up the phone and dial. Even in these situations, however, they can usually ask a friend to help; the friend can stay with them while they talk to a councellor on the phone.

Sometimes teens feel restless, as if they can't stop to do anything, even phone a counsellor. They feel as if they are spinning faster and faster out of control, and that if they stopped, they'd have to confront their emotions, which they are trying to avoid. A friend might understand and help.

Some schools have peer counsellors, students who receive training in counselling. These may be students who have tried suicide themselves and moved past such feelings, or those who are gifted with great compassion and can understand what other teens are feeling. They are available, usually, through the counsellor or, in a small school, by asking friends.

Whoever a teen talks to, talking to someone immediately is very important. Everyone has a need to be understood and accepted, whether it's their parents or not. Rena's parents were shocked at her suicide attempt; they had not known she was so depressed and disturbed. They immediately began talking to her, helping her, trying to understand her. However, only two teens I talked to received more attention from their parents, so, perhaps, expecting parental help is in many cases unrealistic. So long as teens feel they have someone to talk to – parents, friends, counsellors – they can keep their hope alive.

Teens can also develop a support system, as Teresa did, made up of friends, parents of friends, and work-mates – people who cared about her. This kind of support system gives teens a positive image of themselves and makes them feel more worthwhile. And as we all know, self-esteem is vital to a teen's sense of well-being.

### RESOURCES

*She's got to make good*
*got to make good*
*No one wants to listen to the little girl cry*
*The little girl pretends too well*
*too well*
*The little girl can run fast*
*can run faster than anyone*
*She chooses to sit in a wheelchair and cry*
*and cry*
*She's the only one who can help herself*
*who can help*
*Everyone's too busy*
*Everyone.*

– T.S.

Ideally, parents are teens' first resource. When they fail, friends, other family members, counsellors, and other professionals can offer help and support. Often, however, it may be a combination of these, and teens may have to be persistent in order to get the help they need.

Leslie could not go down the stairs to the apartment below and talk to her mother or father, nor did she have any friends she could confide in. So she went to her school counsellor, but she found he was more interested in feeding Leslie's school number into the computer and finding her statistics (her grades, her school absences, her tardiness) than in looking across the desk at the suicidal girl who was crying for help.

When Janet could not talk to her grandparents, she tried the school counsellor. However, the counsellor did not have much ability to counsel. "I spent a lot of time in her office, from the second semester until June, and I didn't get anywhere with her. She was a really nice person but . . . it was really boring. I told her I was a schizophrenic [Janet was not] and she couldn't figure me out. And, like, the counsellor said everything was confidential, but the word got around. So the counsellor told one teacher and she told another one and pretty soon everyone was coming up to me and saying, 'Oh you poor child.' Right? 'Go to hell,' was my answer. I got really mad at her. It shows they care, but I didn't need her talking about me." Janet felt cheated, understandably, since the counsellor was not keeping her confidence.

Teens in trouble should be able to reach a professional through school counsellors or a local mental health association, but it's not always easy. Some teens I talked to lived in small towns, or went to schools where there was only one counsellor whom everyone knew was not good. Even those who lived in urban areas said they still found it hard to get help the first time they tried. Even at the time of their suicide attempt when their need for help was the greatest, some found the hospital staff whom they thought would be understanding, were instead hostile, angry, and not particularly compassionate.

While Tanya and I absorbed the sunshine in the park and the peace and tranquility around us, she told me about her second suicide attempt. She was treated by the same nurse at the hospital as she had had the first time. "The nurse sat down with me and said, 'What the hell's your problem? This is the second time in two months. Do you really think we have the time for you? We need our time for really sick people.' I thought she'd just given me another reason for dying. I said, 'I'm sorry. I'm sorry. I'm sorry for existing.' That's how I felt."

Bruce was in the hospital at age thirteen for attempting suicide. The doctors kept him for four hours, pumped his stomach, then asked him why he did it. He told them that he didn't know why. He was sent home without any follow-up or recommendations for counselling.

Robert was taken to the hospital by a cab driver who could see he was very sick. The hospital phoned his parents, who later sent him to the family doctor. The doctor told him, "This is stupid. Do you realize that you would have been hurting your family if you had killed yourself?"

Robert thought it would have been much better if the doctor had asked him why he did it in the first place. He didn't feel a lecture was good counselling.

But not everyone had a bad experience with health professionals. Beth got help from her family doctor. "She set us [Beth and her family] up with a psychiatrist and we went and saw her. Well, just me. They [her parents] went once, but that was further along." When Beth tried suicide again her mother called the family doctor who then called the psychiatrist. The psychiatrist told her mother to take Beth to the hospital right away. The family doctor suggested the adolescent ward at Vancouver General Hospital.

"So I went there and they talked to me for six hours and tested me and everything and they asked, 'Do you want to enter, to admit yourself? You don't have to.' I said, 'Yes, I do.' I was really scared. I'd drunk a whole bottle of vodka. I threw up a lot.

"They stuck a tube down my throat. I remember that. My mother was seeing an analyst so she had a whole bunch of drugs. Lithium. She used to be on Tranxene and Lithium. I know she has to take one pill to wake herself up in the morning and another to go to bed.

"I went in. At first I was going into the psychiatric assessment unit. And I don't know, I didn't think I was one of them. But I stayed there about a week and then they transferred me to East 2, a teenage unit. There were rooms for two girls or one girl. There were ten of us there. We were all teenagers and everything was done on a point and merit system. In the daytime we had things where we'd work together and talk. We all ate meals together. There was a TV room. We did our own laundry. Every night we had an hour of quiet time and there were psych nurses that would come around and talk to you. They were always there. You saw a doctor every two days or so.

"It was really good. If you ever felt you were going to blow it, they had a room with pads and pillows and a blanket, and it was just for you. There was like a merit system. We were all at Stage 3. There were other, worse, stages where you had to stay in your room, and eat all your meals there. You'd get all your privileges taken away from you. As you imroved you got to go out. You could go out in the hospital grounds, and, better still, you could go off the hospital grounds if they knew exactly where you were going. You could have a day pass or a weekend pass if your doctor felt it was okay.

"The doctor was good. He said, 'It's not Beth's problem. It's the whole family's problem.' So he got the whole family and myself in and gave us advice on communicating better. And I can still go and see him on an outpatient basis. It went along fine for almost a year and then I left home."

Not many got that kind of support and help, but there is help like that out there.

Megan had had what she thought was a pretty good relationship with her social worker. When she attempted suicide by overdosing, the first person she told was the social worker. "I didn't want to tell my mom at the time. And I haven't told her yet. The social worker was all for telling my mom and marching me to the emergency hospital. I didn't want that. I stopped talking to her [the social worker]. I found talking to my friend helped a lot more. The social worker couldn't handle it. And by this time I was trying to talk to my mom more."

Bruce found some help from a corrections officer and some agencies. "The John Howard Society was good. That helped. The Salvation Army was good too, especially during my time at WYO [juvenile detention home]. They're there to lend a hand. They overlook your problems and make you feel at home."

There are no guarantees that teens will get help when they ask for it. Sometimes they hesitated to ask for help because they didn't know how the person they were going to approach would feel. But even if they don't know, teens should know that some people do care; they may even be grateful that the teens trusted them enough to talk to them.

However, some people may feel too uncomfortable or incompetent to deal with the teens' problems, so they try to explain that the problems are not so serious, and that they don't really *need* help. This makes it easier for them not to respond. Troubled teens shouldn't waste energy blaming those who can't help. Look for someone else. There is a network somewhere that will be useful, a group of people who will care and want to help.

## ADVICE FROM TEENS

*I see my reflection*
*As I sit poolside*
*Yet the rippled mirror*
*Shows no more than my features*
*Anyone could look at me now*
*And not know what I've been through.*

– Rena

Many of the teens I interviewed had tried suicide more than once and had lived with the humiliation, rejection, and emotional trauma that had come with their attempts. I asked all of them for any advice they could offer that would help other teens. What did they think other teens in similar circumstances might do? When they looked back on their troubled times, what did they think they should have done differently? How did they manage to overcome their families' negative image of them, and finally begin to feel good about themselves?

They told me that making changes in their lives was important. Sometimes the changes were very small, but each one allowed them to move on. Several made changes in their view of themselves. Leslie said, "I've come to the point where it's me that matters." She had thought that she had to preserve her family, had to be the one who kept everything together. After her suicide attempt she had to go through a very difficult process of talking things out and trying to understand herself, but it was this attitude, *I'm important*, that made a difference to her.

Amy changed her outlook on herself slowly over time. She tried suicide on numerous occasions before finally, when she was about eighteen, she realized that she had grown past a lot of her problems. "I had to give life another chance. There was always something. I knew it would always get better. Things always do. I can talk to my friends now. Suicide didn't do anything." This change of attitude took time and experience; she had to live past the worst of her problems before she believed in herself enough to think she could handle life. No one came by and rescued her. She looked at her life, talked out her problems, and rescued herself.

Teresa found her own strength after several suicide attempts. "After the Anacin bit [a suicide attempt], it was just, like, I had to take my life in my own hands because no one else was going to help. It was like a one-woman crusade type of thing. I was going to be the best I could be and nobody was going to stop me. I don't let people stop me now."

Rena wrote me a letter three months after our interview. She said, "Tell them there *are* people who care. But they can't help alone. You yourself have to let them help.

"The main thing is to feel good about yourself. You're not conceited if you love and respect yourself. Only healthy."

When people tell teens that they should "just buckle down and take charge" of themselves, they don't understand that teens simply can't do that. Not at that moment, anyway. Leslie, Amy, and Teresa had to live through many failures before they found help, strength, direction, and a feeling that they were okay. Once they had that feeling of being worthwhile, important, admirable even, then they could feel they could handle life.

Many of the teens I interviewed advised other teens in trouble to find someone who can help.

Robert said, "Find somebody to talk to. Listen to what he has to say. Don't hang around your parents if they are the cause of your problems. They try to hold on and that's just going to make you worse. My parents don't want me to make mistakes, but I learn better if I do make mistakes. If need be, even run away for a while. Stay with a friend. Find a friend who you can talk to, who will listen to what you have to say. I think if I was faced with it again, I'd probably run away. That seems to be a smarter way, rather than suicide."

Robert did talk to workers at his local crisis center quite a few times. He found them always ready to listen when he needed someone. "The crisis center was so good that they said, 'If things are so bad at home, we can find you a place to stay.' And that was just great. That's what I needed to hear. As long as I had someone to talk to, it was okay. If I didn't have them to talk to I don't know what would have happened. I wouldn't be here right now.

"I called them every week. They wanted me to call and tell them what I'd been going through. There wasn't anyone else. I couldn't talk to my parents. I couldn't talk to my friends because they all thought I was . . . weird. The people at the crisis center were the ones that asked me how I was feeling, what I wanted to do. That's what I liked above anything. Asking me. It was the first time I'd felt important. After my ordeal at the hospital I phoned them up. They didn't say, 'You stupid. Why did you do this?' It was like, 'You must have really needed someone to talk to.' It was so fantastic that someone would understand like that."

Tanya felt the importance of finding someone who would listen. "You have to take the first step and say, 'Hey. I need help!' And if the first person doesn't help you, you have to find somebody else." She told me how hard it was to reach out. "You don't want to admit there's something wrong with you. You know down inside that there is, but you don't want to admit it. You're ashamed. You're really ashamed. You can't handle it." The teens also didn't realize that there were others who felt the same way they did; they thought they were the only ones, or at least the only ones in their school, neighbourhood, or social group. "My dad is really successful in what he does, well-respected," Tanya said. "For me to go to him and say, 'Dad, I can't handle life. . .' I couldn't do it. I had to have somebody go and do it for me."

So many teens thought that they had to handle all their problems by themselves, and many wanted to do it this way. They didn't want to be dependent on anyone, whether it was other kids or professionals. Some others didn't think of accepting help in dealing with their life, or they didn't know how to get help.

Suzanne, fifteen, asked me to pass on her advice. She said to tell other teens, "Remember that there is someone out there, always, even if you have to go looking for them. That's what you really need. Someone to tell you that you're okay."

One of the more interesting groups I came across was Megan's circle of friends. She had three who were loyal and committed to a deep friendship. They went to the same school, listened to each other's problems, and were alert for signs of depression in the others.

"If one of the girls is depressed we'll spend the night with her . . . two of us, or all three of us. Or sometimes, if a girl is depressed, the others will treat her to supper. Like, we'll all chip in and pay for her. If I'm really depressed, the others will pick me up after school. We drop all our books at Tara's house and Tara and me and the other two will go out. It's all okay with our folks. We usually go for pizza. And we'll sit down and order a huge pizza, ham and pineapple, huge pops, and we'll sit there, until it closes at one in the morning, and we'll just talk. It really, really helps a lot.

"Talking about suicide has helped me see that it's final. If someone's depressed we'll talk about it and try to figure out why. Like if I've got a problem, I know they'll say, 'You're not alone.' Sometimes when one of us is really depressed and I ask them why, and they say, 'Oh, because I got a bad grade on my test,' and we can tell, like, that's not the truth. So we'll go out together and talk until we figure out why."

I asked if they ever got into things they couldn't handle.

"I think if I were by myself, I'd feel that way. But because there are three of us listening, we just keep talking until we help."

Since most teens told me that they wouldn't talk to adults, or they didn't know any adults they could talk to, Megan's mutual caring group seems to be a great way to deal with problems. If teens have tried suicide in the past, they are better able to understand someone else's preoccupation with it. They can see the problems that others ignore and can help because they, after all, have been through it too and managed to stay alive.

Many teens told me that they felt they had to help others at school, even teens they barely knew, when they saw that they were depressed or when they realized that those students were thinking about suicide. Teens who had tried suicide were unlikely to assume that the worries of those students weren't serious, and so didn't ridicule them, or put them down with sarcasm or jokes. They understood and were able to help and proved to be powerful friends. Sometimes another teen is all the help a suicidal teen has. Since suicide is the second most frequent cause of death in teenagers, and teenagers see other teens as their first lifeline, they are very important to each other.

Some teens run into the problem of the "deadly secret." A teen confides his suicidal plans and asks that his friend tell no one. The friend worries that he will try suicide, yet at the same time, she worries that if she "tells" his parents or a teacher, the teen will deny it, telling everyone that she is lying and generally creating a mess. But if someone confides that he is thinking of suicide, the friend must assume that the part of him that wants to live is asking for help, and get some.

David told me that he felt he had more options as he grew older. That, of course, is true. With time, teens have more ability to get out into the community, more contacts with helping agencies, more freedom to come and go, and a better chance of a job and perhaps more money to do things than they did when they were younger, but it doesn't necessarily mean they won't have suicidal thoughts unless they have dealt with their problems, or their problems have diminished. Sometimes just living through problems makes teens understand that they have a lot of inner strength, but sometimes time doesn't give them those answers. They still have the same problems with parents whether they are sixteen or thirty-six. The low self-esteem may still be there; they may still feel unimportant and unwanted.

Many of the teens I interviewed felt alone, ignored, and invisible in society, but I was impressed by the many people who did care about them. The teens who answered my newspaper ad wanted to help others. Crisis center personnel and other professionals really wanted to do something to help. We all want teens to believe that there is someone near who cares, there is someone who will help. Teens in trouble need to keep trying until they find that someone.

# FOUR

## *The Parent's Role*

*When i turn out the light*
*and go to bed*
*i lie hoping for a new and better tomorrow*
*But thoughts of reality creep from the shadows*
*in which i try to keep them hidden*
*during the brightness of my days.*
*They tell me there are no promises, no guarantees*
*and no assurances. There is emptiness, loneliness,*
*fear, guilt, shame*
*And i allow no tears, though they do want me*
*Tomorrow is new but*
*will it bring peace and laughter and acceptance.*
*i will get lost in tomorrow,*
*like today, like yesterday.*
*i will cry where no one can see – inside.*
*and drown a little more beneath those tears. i will*
*hold them tightly and safely, and will not let them go*
*like i wish someone would do to me.*

*– Tanya*
(adapted from a longer poem)

## HOW PARENTS CAN HELP

The stories teens told me about their decision to try suicide often re-
volved around their parents. Parents were significant figures in their lives
and their decisions. This crucial role can be overwhelming to parents.
They are not magicians or extraordinarily talented psychologists. Even
though parents try to be responsive to teens, obviously, in many cases, this
is not enough. Parents need to better understand the seriousness of what

their child is going through. They also need to know that their child's fear of rejection, and their need for their parents' help, are real.

It came as a surprise to me when teens said that their parents were the most important people in their lives. In some ways this was gratifying, but in other ways, terrifying. If parents are that important to teens, how do we, the imperfect, well-meaning, ordinary people without professional training, help our children? With common sense and love? Yes, but teens need more than that. They need our understanding, and I found that understanding particularly difficult. I had not even thought of suicide as something my own children might think about. Considering the statistical evidence that says that it definitely is an option for teens, why did I not pay serious attention to this? Why don't other parents consider the possibility of suicide seriously?

Some parents are understandably overwhelmed by the amount of knowledge and skill they need to raise a child. To keep a child safe, a parent has to teach not only honesty, diligence, responsibility, and caring, but safe sex, the dangers of sexual predators, how to floss teeth, treat acne, ski and swim safely, and avoid being mugged in the park or raped on the beach.

The expectation of being "super-mom" and "super-dad" can be crushing. It is easier to deny that our children have any risk of suicide than it is to take on another packet of information and another teaching task.

Today, many parents struggle to pay for books, clothes, food, education, music lessons, orthodontic work, and school trips. Often parents use most of their energy working to maintain their families financially, and have little energy or time to devote to their kids. The days are gone when parents spent hours each day with their children doing house chores, preparing and sharing meals, and simply being together. Today, parents and teens don't spend the kind of "quality" time together where wisdom and advice can be imparted causally and easily. These days parents often have to make an appointment with their teens, sometimes days in advance, to spend an hour with them. And then, or course, there is the time that parents need without the children in order to keep their marriages together.

The conflicting and difficult demands on parents' time make it hard for them to meet their teens' needs. But the teens do have needs. As young people with little experience, they are less equipped to deal with life than their parents, and they need help. Parents who are aware of the possibility of suicide and who know the signs that the teen is considering it are better able to help.

## How Parents View Teens

It is difficult for parents to step back from their families and take an objective look at the relationships that cause them to act and react the way they do. When they take this step, their view may be complicated by the ties that bind them to other family members. But if they can do so, they can get a better understanding of how difficult life is for their teens and try to assess the danger to their life.

It is often hard to define the problems of teenagers. Parents may sense that their teens are worried or anxious or angry, but be completely ignorant about why they are like that. It is important to look at what the teens are doing and to try to assess what that means, whether their actions are escape strategies or something else.

### ALCOHOL

While many teens use alcohol as their parents do, i.e., only during weekend parties surrounded by friends, some use alcohol as an habitual escape. The difference between social drinking and antisocial drinking is usually only one of degree. They may have similar motivations, but most people manage without alcohol except on certain occasions, while teens escaping into alcohol use it often. They may be able to cope with life *only* if they are under alcohol's influence. This is not only a drinking problem, it is also a symptom of low self-esteem and self-destructive ideas. Alcoholism can develop very quickly in teens, moving them from occasional drinking to compulsive drinking within weeks.

### OTHER DRUGS

For many teens, drugs provide a similar escape. Drugs are usually easy to get and some, such as crack cocaine, are inexpensive. Using drugs can be a pleasurable escape that is entirely at the will and control of the teen. Those who have never used drugs may not understand the seductive power of the pleasure they produce, and some may try them again in order to experience those euphoric and omnipotent feelings over and over. A teen may use drugs initially to escape, but as with alcohol addiction, may quickly become habituated or addicted.

### TELEVISION

Television is often used as an escape from reality. Many teens spend hours every day watching the fantasy world of sitcoms, drama, and now (ironically) reality shows. The plots of the stories replace the problems of the real world until television becomes the teens' reality. Teens don't have to think about their own problems until the show is over, or until the next program is over, or the next one. This delays their need to have to face their problems or make any decisions. Teens who suffer from depression or an inability to cope with life stretch out these periods of escape to the point where they are watching television most of the day and night.

### MUSIC

Loud music occupies the mind and temporarily drives out reality. I take a cassette to the dentist, put the headphones on, and the countermelody in a brass ensemble successfully blocks out the anxieties I have about dentistry. Music serves somewhat the same purpose for teens. They can concentrate on the music and block out painful reality. Teen culture promotes music that is not necessarily enjoyed by adults or young children; the music is theirs and not understood or tolerated by other age groups. This keeps teens isolated from adults, including parents, and allows them another means of escape.

### SKIPPING SCHOOL

A study indicated that forty percent of teens are not in school the day before they try suicide. Certainly, many of the teens I talked to only intermittently attended school. As one girl said, "I didn't feel like going to class. That becomes a habit, too. Like, I didn't do the homework I was supposed to from the class I missed last week, so I'd better not go to class this week either." The problems that are raised by missing classes compound the problems the teen is already experiencing, and school becomes just one more source of tension. When looking for a way to escape this tension, skipping school seems a reasonable option.

### SELF-INJURY

Many teens who have low self-esteem and are considering the possibility of suicide feel compelled to injure themselves. Several I talked to used a knife to carve slash marks on themselves – their arms, their stomachs. In many cases, these scars were ignored by their parents. One girl showed me long scars on the inside of her arms which she had had for years, but her parents had never asked her about them. It doesn't take a psychology degree to understand that a teen who mutilates herself has such low self-esteem she thinks she deserves to be hurt, but it may take a psychologist to help parents deal with it. Parents may think that if they don't pay any attention to slash scars, their child will stop injuring herself. But parents still need to help teens with the the underlying problem that made slashing seem like a good idea in the first place. Sometimes teens find help outside the family, but sometimes ignoring such mutilations will prompt teens to repeat or increase their self-destructive behaviour. Not talking about it tells the teens that their parents don't care, that their clear call for help is being ignored.

### PREVIOUS ATTEMPTS

All attempts by teens to harm themselves must be taken seriously, even those that are obvious "attention getters," since these are strong cries for help and often come before a fatal attempt.

If a parent sees a daughter taking twelve headache pills, the daughter is demonstrating many feelings she can't or won't articulate, including her attraction to suicide. Teens often act out what they cannot say. Many who attempt suicide are trying to communicate their emotions as much as, if not more than, they are trying to die. Still, parents need to accept the fact that this is an attempt at suicide.

The anger, frustration, and helplessness that parents feel at such a time make it difficult for them to focus on what help their teenager needs. It's dangerous to dismiss such attempts as "only an attention getter," or to justify their lack of action by telling themselves that if she were serious about dying she would have taken more pills. She *is* serious about dying; she demonstrated this by her actions.

There is a myth that those who try suicide with the obvious intention of being stopped by friends or relatives will never kill themselves. This is not true. Those who have already attempted suicide in any fashion are quite likely to commit the fatal act. A teen who has made a suicide attempt needs immediate family help and support and the entire family needs counselling and professional help to get through this crisis. Parents need to be convinced that any suicide attempt is a "wake-up call" and has given them time and a chance to help their child.

### THE TYRANNY OF THREATS

In some cases, teens know that their parents are so upset by their threats of suicide that their parents will do almost anything for them. These are the teens who use threats to control their parents: "If you don't let me go to the dance, I'll kill myself," or "Everyone else has a Porsche. If you don't get me a Porsche, I'll jump off the school roof." It is rarely possible for parents in these situations to extradite themselves and their teens without harm.

In these cases, parents' concerns about suicide contribute to the teens' manipulative ploys. But parents can't afford to ignore these threats, because lack of concern about threats of suicide is dangerous. The family needs professional diagnostic help and supportive treatment from a psychiatrist, psychologist, or family counsellor. Parents need the psychiatrist as much as the teens do, because they require guidance in order to navigate through this potentially dangerous situation.

## Family and Friends

It may seem to some parents that teens are not influenced by family at all. Many teens seem uninterested in or reluctant to join family outings. Yet the teens I talked to consistently told me that their families mattered to them, and that their relationship with their parents was more important than any other. They reached out by developing ties with girlfriends and boyfriends, but these new friends did not make their need for a strong relationship with their parents any less important.

Teens need to hear, repeatedly, that they are valued, accepted, and appreciated by their parents. They do not assume they are loved; in fact, they very often assume they are not.

Parents often show little faith in their teens' abilities to cope and give countless admonitions and directions which reinforce the teens' fear that they cannot cope. The parents' motivation is to help their teens by showing them the "right" way. But the teens interpret direction and criticism as a lack of faith and trust: "You tell me what to do all the time. You don't think I can think anything out for myself."

It is sometimes difficult for teens to receive support from family because they are geographically far away. In such instances, families can make sure reliable role models are available for their children by appointing trusted friends or relatives. Teens may go to these contacts for consultation and support when they can't talk to their parents.

Such outside support as friends and relatives can be valuable as they are often uncritical and supportive. They may also have spent years getting to know the teen during outings, vacations, and social occasions. Teens who spend time with someone who knows them and admires them promotes confidence and self-esteem.

If the family has moved many times, it's hard to be sure that the children have longstanding relationships with friends or relatives. It is still crucial for the teen to have a circle of reliable adult friends. Over and over, teens told me they needed someone to listen to them. If they are in the habit of talking to friends or relatives, they will have someone who will listen. Parents need to think about their family circle, their social circle, and their teens' social circle. Is there anyone they feel is a friend? Do the teens spend much time with this friend?

## Separating From the Family

We often complain that we cannot reach our teens, that they are emotionally distant from us because that's the way the kids want it. However, parents may have indicated to teens that they don't want them in the family any longer, that it is time they left. In anticipation of teens leaving home, parents may force separation on them before they are ready. We may send our son out to get a job before he is capable, or send our daughter off to find an apartment before she can cope, making them responsible for serious decisions before they feel they can manage.

Sometimes parents force rules on their teens – you will not go out with those friends, you will be in by ten o'clock, you will get better grades – that are the criteria for remaining in the family. When parents do this, they force the teen to choose between dependence (you will do as you are told) or isolation (you will leave home). This is a very difficult position for teens to be in. Outside influences are strong and usually not controlled by parents. Some parents have been so involved in their children's lives that they cannot accept the fact that they are no longer the organizers and directors of their teens' lives. They try to continue the patterns that served them in those earlier years. This inability on the part of parents to give their teens room to grow and experience disappointment and failure that comes with experience often results in a directive that is an ultimatum: "Either you obey our rules or you leave home." For the teens there is often no choice at all: either they are dependent and accepted, or defiant and isolated.

Sometimes parents do not make the choice obvious, but instead withdraw emotionally from their teens until the choice becomes isolation without emotional support at home (unless the teens are obedient), or isolation without emotional support away from home. This tactic of control by parents only makes the relationship worse.

The task of the teens is to separate from the family while still feeling emotionally supported. By demanding compliance, insisting that teens do as they are told, parents can force isolation on the teen. Certainly, teens are unlikely to confide in their parents under these conditions; they can't afford to be honest and straightforward with parents who want to control them. Parents often have trouble deciding in what areas they need to relinquish control and what areas they must retain control. Boundaries shift quickly and dramatically in the teen years, and parents must continually reassess what kind of decisions and responsibilities they are willing to leave to their teen.

The task of the teens separating from the family is paralleled by the reciprocal task of parents separating from the teens. We may have as much trouble letting go as the teen has in going. It is hard to give up control of your children's lives, especially if they are making what parents see as bad choices.

It is tempting to lean even harder on teens who are failing in school or who are in other ways making poor choices. Parents must remember that failure is part of the process of learning and that teens need to experience it. When teens make mistakes, parents may be tempted to want to take control of their lives again; they find it difficult to allow teens to experience failure and to allow them to deal with it on their own terms. The key is to let go of the teens in stages, a little at a time, until they reach full independence.

## Outside Influences

Parents often assess their teens' friends by their activities; for example, a basketball group is a good influence and a partying group is a bad influence.

Many parents assume that teens who are socializing with the basketball team, debating club, high school yearbook staff, and the high school band are stable, active, and socially happy. Teens say this is not necessarily so.

Many who contemplate suicide manage a façade of multiple activities that mask their difficulties. They may have the appearance of being busy and well-adjusted, but they may also have standards of perfection they can't possibly achieve and, in spite of achievements, feel like a failure. This contributes to their low self-esteem and, despite all that parents would assume to the contrary, they may be unhappy and depressed.

It is not so much what teens' activities are as how they feel about themselves that is significant, and whether they can talk about those feelings with anyone. Parents need to assess the teens' interactions with their friends. Do they listen to each other? Good friends, male and female, consult constantly about many things. They need time to talk. Are the teens' lives organized so that they have that time to talk?

Parents may feel at a loss to know what is normal teenage behaviour and what is a warning sign for suicide. They often don't know how to deal with teens who have grown up in a culture different and more complicated from the one they grew up in. Are their teens undisciplined when they disagree with a parent, or is this a sign of healthy independence?

## What Parents Can Do

Parents sometimes feel that if they could just change a few things in their teens' lives — grades, friends, bestow ambition, drive, or courtesy — then all would be well. But parents have no power to make changes in anyone but themselves, and that is where parents should spend some effort. Sometimes changes will occur in other people in the family as they react to the change in the parents, but the only ones parents can count on changing are themselves.

It is often difficult for parents to understand the changes in their teens that they cannot control — how the children they reared have grown into strangers. Parents cannot change their teen's behaviour if they don't understand the feelings that motivate them in the first place. By assessing their families and themselves, parents can become more aware of what they do, and learn to understand how they affect others within the family. They need to understand better why they act the way they do.

## MISGUIDED HELP

Parents often give advice and try to help their teens by pointing out what the teens should have done in certain situations. But if unchecked, such advice may evolve into constant criticism, the effect of which, as noted earlier, can be severe. The teens feel rejected. Parents may criticize because they believe:

- the teens will remain with the family if the parents continually treat them like a child;
- the teens will need the parents to always guide them, and the parents sees no other role for themselves other than as models of authority and guidance;
- the teens will listen to the parents and remain safe from the troubles of the world;
- the teens will listen to the parents and avoid failure;
- it seems less risky to the parents to take out their anger and frustration about other issues (e.g., work, marriage) on the teens than on other adults.

These are common reasons parents criticize, but not the only ones. Constantly criticizing their teens results in some kind of satisfaction for the parents, or they would not do it.

It is common for parents to say that the reason they can't deal with their teens is because of some fault in the teens – e.g., they are lazy, selfish, useless, or have some other character flaw – and that if they just faced up to this fact, things would improve. It is hard for parents to admit that they don't always like their teens; in fact, many parents blame their teens for the mutual dislike: "If he'd just go to school, I could like him"; "If she'd just get a job, I'd like her."

The worst aspect of this situation is that teens believe their parents are setting up impossible goals that they cannot achieve, and that no matter what they do, their parents will hate them because, fundamentally, they are no good. Once teens accept their parents' assessment of being "no good," then they feel they don't deserve life or happiness.

## SENSITIVITY TO REJECTION

Not all teens who are rejected by their parents will commit suicide. Some may leave home, or throw themselves into education or a career, or even join a cult where they feel accepted. But most teens who commit suicide feel rejected by their parents. Parents often do not believe they are rejecting their teens by their actions. Most would say they love their teens even if they don't approve of them, don't want them around, and constantly criticize them, but this is not the message the teens hear.

It is possible for parents to feel responsible for teens, worry about them, financially support them, but still reject them. Rejection is obvious to teens – they understand it instinctively and usually assess it accurately – but it is less obvious to parents. Parents often prefer not to admit to it and have ways of denying such feelings to themselves. But it is not the parents' view of emotional support that is important here; it is the teens' perspectives that matter. It is their understanding of rejection that affects them. If they feel rejected, they suffer whatever the parents' expressed feelings are.

A forgiving twenty-year-old woman told me, "When I tried suicide last time, the reasons were different from the reasons I had the first time. Last time I was severely depressed and I felt I had nobody. There was nobody there. My parents didn't give me what I needed. It wasn't that they weren't trying; it was that they didn't know how. They didn't know what I was going through."

This statement gave me concern because either this young woman was denying that her parents were indifferent, or her parents, in spite of trying, could not understand her despair.

Teens often do feel isolated from their parents. An eighteen-year-old told me, "My parents never take time to do things with me. My dad works about sixteen hours a day, eats dinner, goes to his bedroom. My mother, she used to be a lot better, but in the last year, she's started doing the same thing. She works for a long time, comes home, makes dinner, goes into the bedroom with my dad. They sit there and watch TV. They sit there in one world, and I'm in another."

Teresa said, "Friends of mine say they did it [tried suicide] because their parents wouldn't listen. Nobody would listen to them. Maybe we're going through typical teenaged problems, but it hits some people more severely than some parents think. Parents don't see it. It's like parents think those problems are normal. Well, they're not normal. Problems can get pretty heavy. Especially with the kind of people you get mixed up with. On more than one occasion I've been in over my head and nobody's been there to help me out. Some kids say, 'Oh, I can go to my mom.' Ten to one they couldn't if they really needed her. I bet they couldn't.

"I would have loved to sit and talk to my mother and tell her what was going on. But I was so afraid because of the reactions I'd gotten be-fore. I mean, I'd like to have told her, 'Look, Mom, sex is getting to be a problem for me. I don't know what's right for me.' But if I even men-tioned the word, she would have freaked."

Teens judge the degree of rejection not only by what parents say, but by their attitudes and actions. It is necessary for parents to make those attitudes and actions supportive ones.

## Changing Parental Habits

Parents may find it difficult to change their behaviour patterns. Some-times it may seem that their brains and their mouths are not connected; their minds tell them not to criticize at the same time they hear them-selves doing it. As most of us know, it is very hard to change our habits. We had reasons for our original actions and attitudes, but whatever they were, parents need to remember that whatever we say to teens affects them profoundly.

Teens' problems often come at a time when parents are preoccu-pied with a great many difficulties of their own: mortgages, educational funds, clothing bills, their marriages. They may need counselling them-selves in order to deal with their own overwhelming problems. It may be that they can't work on improving relationships with their teens until they have done this.

While it is probable that the possibility of teen suicide is not the only problem in the family, it is the one that needs immediate attention. In their efforts to understand why their teen might choose suicide, par-ents need to look at what actions of theirs might be contributing to that choice.

TIME

Dealing with teens can take up a lot of parents' time. This can come as quite a shock to parents who think teens are usually away from home, at friends' places, at the movies, at school, or doing their homework. In fact, they can take hours out of one's day.

But it is necessary; even the most independent teens need time to talk, even if it is about what they did that day. No one is ever completely independent of the need for others — everyone needs to feel supported and accepted. The better teens feel about themselves, the more independent they are, but they still need to know that the lines of communication are open.

Making that time can be one of the most difficult aspects of raising teens. The problem is that teens need parental guidance according to the crises in their lives. Whatever the amount, parents need to make themselves available to their teens when it is needed. The teen crisis won't wait.

## Listening

Teens told me that at the time they tried suicide they felt they could not talk about their feelings to anyone, that there was no one who would listen, no one who cared. They said all they wanted was someone to listen uncritically and nonjudgmentally. This does not seem an impossible request, but I understand why it is difficult for parents to hear their teens' problems without immediately offering advice, direction, censure, sympathy, comfort, and a plan for change. It is extremely hard just to listen.

One eighteen-year-old girl told me how she failed to get her parents to listen to her the first time she tried to kill herself.

"I bandaged everything up and my dad, he's Dutch and he's disciplined and dominating, he comes in and says, 'What did you do?' My mom's crying. He said, 'What did you do?' I told him and he said, 'Show me.' And I showed him, and he said, 'Not good enough!' I always remember that. He walked off and said, 'If you wanted to kill yourself, you would have done a better job.'"

While you might be able to defend the father's logic, one cannot defend his lack of compassion. It could well be that the father in this instance was trying to convince himself that his daughter did not want to die because *he* did not want her to die. Perhaps he did love her and could not face the idea that she wanted to die, but his daughter was convinced that he despised her because she had failed in a suicide attempt, and that she should make sure she completed the task the next time she tried.

The constant shifting of priorities can be hard to manage. Parents need to remind themselves that listening time with their teens is vitally important, and remember that, like all parents, they may easily underrate the importance of some crises, and overrate the importance of others.

Many parents may not find it easy to listen to their teens. Parents can make wonderful confidants for other people's children, but find it hard to listen with that same empathy to their own. Some parents feel that when their teen offers information about school problems, sex, or drugs, the parents have to do something about it, that it is the parents' responsibility to intervene in some way in the teen's life.

For the most part, parents need only to listen. But parents also need to convey interest in their teens' lives. Many parents convey indifference, hostility, criticism, even contempt by the way they interact with their teens. Listening, to be beneficial, must be a warm, comfortable process in which the teens feel understood, accepted, and supported. This requires the parents to keep in mind some firm rules:

- Do not offer advice. If they do, they are denying the teens the chance to work out the problem for themselves. And parents may give the wrong advice since they may not have all the facts. The teen may then be reluctant to talk about the problem again.
- Do not criticize, even mildly. There is nothing that stops conversation so completely and so dramatically as criticism.
- Do not compare teens with others. There is always someone better. How would parents like to be compared to Tom Cruise or Britney Spears in looks, Albert Einstein in intelligence, or Leonardo da Vinci in talent? There is always someone, even close to home, who is more accomplished, more talented, and more hard-working than you are. The teens may already be suffering from feelings of incompetence; they don't come to talk to their parents in order to feel worse.
- Do not mitigate or exaggerate the problem. If parents tell their teens that the problem isn't as bad as it seems, either the teens won't believe them or they will feel foolish. It is different for teens to discover, after talking out a problem, that it isn't as bad as first thought, than to be told that the problem is minor. and if parents exaggerate or make too much of the problem, the teens will wish they'd never opened their mouths.
- Do not sympathize. Many parents think that by offering sympathy to their teens they are offering support. Sympathy does not support; it is inhibiting. It forces teens to concentrate on how bad they feel, not on the problem.

Sympathy is like a blanket thrown over the problem that prevents teens from picking it up and looking at it. There is quite a difference between saying, "That must be hard for you," which shows empathy and respect, and "You poor darling. I don't see how you can manage." The first comment recognizes the difficulty, but implies faith in the teens to deal with it. The second comment implies that they cannot deal with it at all.

- Express only understanding and acceptance. While this seems very simple when read on the page, it is not so easy in practice, especially if you are in the habit of acting differently.

OPPORTUNITIES TO LISTEN

Some parents may find that after they have decided that they must be more open to their teens, must be available to them, must listen better, they find that the teens are unresponsive; disappearing into their school and social life, watching TV, stopping periodically in front of the fridge or behind the bathroom door. There never seems to be an opportunity to sit and listen. They don't want to talk.

If parents are having difficulty finding an opportunity to talk, they need to make a date with the teens for lunch at a restaurant, a walk, bowling, or some activity that allows them to be alone together.

While parents might be able to create a receptive atmosphere at home, there may be too many negative associations there to make it possible. The home is parental turf where parents have "ruled." Teens may have habitual reactions in their homes: evasion, resentment, withdrawal. They may find it easier to shed these reactions outside the familial nest. It is also easier for parents to concentrate when they are out of the home and not distracted by mundane tasks and activities.

If the teens' experience has been that time spent with the parent leaves them feeling inadequate ("shitty" is the word I've heard most), then they will avoid their parents, since they don't trust the parents' intentions. Avoiding them is a reasonable protective attitude. But, in spite of their evasive tactics, teens tell me they want a relationship with their parents. Generally, if parents make the effort, teens will eventually give them a chance.

## THE AGENDA

When parents finally get together with their teens, they shouldn't necessarily expect anything but their physical presence. The purpose of this time spent is not so parents can force their teens to talk, but so they can give their teens their attention. Talking, opening the lines of communication, may come later.

Parents shouldn't set an agenda for this time together, nor decide that in this time their teens are going to do or say anything, since their reactions are not within the parents' control. Parents are responsible only for *their* actions and *their* emotions. These outings should be pleasant – not necessarily deep and meaningful. The parents' objective should be to convince their teens that they like them as they are.

## HABITS OF COMMUNICATION

Parents and teens may have developed discouraging patterns of conversation that are difficult to change. With the best intentions parents may find themselves asking questions that they swore they would not – "How's your French mark?" for instance – when the parents know that French is the teen's worst subject. The teen's reaction will probably be, "You know it's my worst subject. You're telling me I'm stupid." Of course, this wasn't the parents' intention. They didn't want their teen to feel stupid, but reassurance that the teen wasn't failing French. To the teen, though, it felt like an attack. Conversation ceases.

When parents try to change their non-helpful habits, they will often say something they would love to retract. The trick is to learn to recognize comments like that before they are said, then refrain from saying them. Apologies may be in order.

It is easier for parents to change their habits when their attitude to their teens change. Parents will find that old comments gradually disappear from conversation and new, positive ones become more habitual. Parents should be forgiving of themselves; change like this takes repeated practice.

## GETTING RID OF BARRIERS TO COMMUNICATION

If parents have seen themselves as their children' guides and protectors, it is difficult for them to accept a more passive supporting role. Acceptance and support do not represent indifference. It takes more time and energy than might be expected to be supporting, non-interfering parents. It also requires a new vocabulary. Parents need to delete from their language sentences that begin with: You ought to. . . . Why don't you. . . . Have you tried. . . . Most kids your age. . . . When I was your age. . . . You need to. . . . You should. . . . You must. . . .

Such statements expose parents' mistrust of their teens' ability to cope by telling them that they need their advice, that they can't manage on their own, that they are incompetent. Any statement from parents that criticizes, judges, directs, or implies an interrogation undermines the teens' faith in themselves.

## NAME-CALLING

Some parents fall into the habit of verbally abusing their teens with negative name-calling: "You're lazy," "You're careless," "You're a failure." If done repeatedly, teens will begin to believe it is true.

Parents often don't think they are so powerful in their children's lives that they can negatively label them and cause them to live up to that label, but they are, so the teens told me. Parents may tell their teens they are lazy so they will work harder, but instead the teens believe their parents' evaluation and accept the fact they are lazy. Such name-calling is one of the most destructive habits that parents have.

## TEACHING

A psychologist told me that he considered one of the worst things parents of teens could do, worse than name-calling, was to lecture them. Lecturing, he thought, was harder on teens — more demoralizing, destructive, demeaning — than any other controlling tactic parents used.

In some families, when parents start to lecture, teens argue back, say nothing at all, or even walk away. In any event, the teens stop listening. Lecturing is thus an ineffective tool when communicating with teens. We usually have vast experience at being lectured ourselves, but somehow that still doesn't make us aware of how ineffective it is.

## PRAISE

It is difficult to understand how praise could possibly hurt teens, but it can be manipulative. Consider what effects the following statement could have: "Your straight As are absolutely wonderful. Look, neighbour, my daughter has straight As. Isn't she wonderful?" The teen believes she is wonderful only when she gets straight As.

When teens tell parents about their accomplishments, parents need to share their sense of pride without dishing out praise as if the achievement were the only thing the parents liked about them.

Many parents were exposed to the theory that parents should praise the "good" behaviour in children and ignore the "bad" in order to control how they behaved. This was an improvement over the method of spanking children for bad behaviour, as the generation before us practiced, but praising good and ignoring bad is still a method of manipulating and controlling behaviour which, however appropriate for young children, is doomed to failure in teens. Teens resent being manipulated, even by praise. And they resist it.

It is one thing for parents to tell their son when he has found the answer to a difficult math problem that he must feel good about that, and another to tell him he is always so wonderful at school. The latter comment can make him feel very uncomfortable; he may know he isn't always wonderful at school, and worry that his parents might expect more than he can give, or that they expect him to do equally well on every test. Teens may feel that parents praise them in order to manipulate them or praise them at inappropriate times, suggesting that their parents don't understand them.

### AGREEMENT

Parents who always agree with their teens isn't a wise path either. Parents can accept the fact that their teens feel a certain way, recognize that they have chosen to deal with a problem one way, and give them emotional support for their choice ("That must have been hard to decide, but I think you can deal with it"), without necessarily agreeing with that choice. Across-the-board agreement can be seen by teens in much the same light as praise; they may believe that it is manipulative. Support, on the other hand, is seen as an emotional plus. Teens realize that you can support their choices without necessarily agreeing with them.

### HOW TO COMMUNICATE

If the above examples are ways *not* to communicate with teens, what are some good ways to communicate? It is surprising how little parents need to say in order to convey understanding.

If parents find it difficult to think of nonjudgmental comments to make to their teens, they might keep in mind a few standby comments, such as "Tell me about it," that will encourage teens to talk. Letting teens speak their mind can show acceptance and support.

The following comments can also be useful, but be aware that they can also act as barriers to communication if used insincerely or inappropriately:

- "Others feel this way, too."
- "I'm sure you can handle this."
- "I know you are capable."
- "What are you going to do about that?"
- "Are you happy with your decision?"
- "Do you want to talk about it?"
- "This is important to you."
- "I'd like to know how you feel."
- "Your point of view is different from mine, and it's interesting to hear how you feel about things."

Parents should try to have the intention of accepting and trying to understand their teens no matter what they say. The objective in taking time to be with teens is not to change, guide, or manipulate them (for their own good), but to listen and understand.

Teens have an incredibly accurate radar for their parents' intentions. They often know what they are, even when the intentions are obscure to the parents themselves.

POWER TRIPS

Some parents have invested years in the process of controlling their children and have no idea how to deal with a child who suddenly will not be controlled. In their efforts to maintain the status quo, parents devise increasingly stronger methods of trying to maintain control while their children devise more and more ways of evading it. Discipline may escalate from the occasional slap to physical abuse, or from the occasional heated word to constant belittling.

I was surprised to learn how many parents tried to force their teens into obedience through hitting. All the teens I talked to who had been hit repeatedly (fifteen of the thirty) had reached an age (between thirteen and eighteen) when they refused to take physical abuse any more, and they either hit back or threatened court action. They were all able to stop their parents from hitting them.

Most parents – even parents who hit their children, impose punishments, and yell and scream – want to help their children. They want them to be happy and productive. Most parents are looking for ways to help their teens and often feel frustrated because nothing seems to work. Most parents would do almost anything to keep their teen safe.

At the very great risk of oversimplifying, I repeat that the best way to help is to listen.

## What Do Parents Want?

What kind of a relationship do parents want with their teens? They may not be able to control what kind of relationship they have – they are not the only ones in the relationship – although it might be helpful to decide what kind of a relationship they truly want.

If parents feel that they can't maintain a close relationship with their teens, they need to decide what they can manage and how they can ensure that their teens receive the support they need from someone else, if not from them. If the parents can't listen, if they find they are becoming too angry or too frustrated, if they cannot resist giving directions or criticism, they need to enlist the help of a friend or relative who can listen. Do the teens have grandparents, aunts, uncles, or cousins who are talented listeners? If the parents cannot help their teens immediately, they need to ask someone else to do so.

## Learning From Teens

Relationships between parents and teens change as the teens get older. Parents should be prepared to learn from them, as they are no longer considered all-knowing, wise, and omnipotent by their teens. Parents can't know all there is to know about life as teens experience it. The problems are different today than when the parents were teens themselves and the solutions often are beyond the parents' experience. Teens are in fact in a position to educate their parents in many areas. This is often difficult for parents to appreciate.

Parents may have relied on their children's belief in their omnipotence in order to maintain their own self-esteem. The child's emerging, more realistic view of parents as fallible humans who make mistakes and have gaps in their knowledge may be harder for parents to accept than it is for children. Parents may feel less important when their teens no longer think they are perfect.

## Letting Go

When parents form the intention of trying to appreciate and listen to their teens rather than trying to change them, it relieves them of a great deal of pressure – although many are not comfortable with this. They feel that they should be trying to change their teens. It helps if parents start to learn the process of letting go a little at a time – to determine that, just for this one outing, this one lunch, this one movie date, they will relinquish their role as prime directors in their teens' lives, and listen.

## Supporting Teens

It amazes me that some children don't realize how much their parents care about them. It seems obvious to me that if we feed, cloth, chauffeur, listen to, advise, urge, question, and admonish our teens, they will understand that we love them. But this cannot be assumed; children need more explicit support. They need to hear, "You are great. You are a fine person. You are a delight."

Many parents are not comfortable with terms of endearment; they think telling a child, "I think you are great," is sentimental and unnecessary. But from the teen's point of view, it is essential to their emotional well-being.

## Magical Repairs to Relationships

Sometimes it is difficult for parents to persevere in efforts to reach their teens when they are met with rejection. Transforming a judgmental, critical, adversarial relationship into a helping, supportive one takes time. Parents cannot feed their teens a magic vitamin and have them be everything they want in a teen. Nor can parents send their teens to finishing schools and have them come home loving, dutiful, and obedient. It simply won't happen.

This generation of parents has their own version of a magic bullet. It seems to lean toward the use of professional counsellors. Many parents believe that if you send your teens and their problems to a counsellor once a week for a year, they will be fixed. A year's worth of counselling may help the teens, but it may not. It is no substitute for parental attention and support.

## When to Start Listening

There is no perfect time to start listening. Whenever the time comes, communication will probably be difficult and somewhat awkward. One teen I know has a masterful technique of saying absolutely nothing when he doesn't want to talk. It is extremely difficult to hold a conversation with a teen who simply won't respond. If parents attempt to schedule a "heart to heart" conversation with their teens, it is far easier to conduct it during another activity, like eating lunch or bowling.

Parents can make a difference over time in their relationships with their teens. They can help to improve their teens' feelings of competence and their perception of their own worth. Teens who attempt suicide usually feel inadequate and unloved, so it is vitally important that parents show their teens that they have faith in them and that they care. They need to do this continually and consistently.

## PARENTS' CHANGING VIEW OF TEENS

As children grow up, they take their view of the world from their families; if they are accepted and supported by them, then they will believe their family's opinion of the world and of themselves. But when children become teens, they begin to see their place in society, and peers and adults outside their families now influence their opinion of themselves. If society has designated them second class because of race, religion, appearance, gender, or sexual orientation, it will have a negative impact on the teens' sense of self-worth. Teens who have been isolated or persecuted by society are particularly vulnerable to thoughts of suicide. It's hard to maintain a healthy belief in their own worth when strangers make nasty remarks about their skin colour, when the guidance counsellor at school thinks they couldn't make an academic program because "your people don't," or when the teacher pulls them aside and asks them not to declare their sexual orientation because it might offend someone. Prejudice appears in both subtle and blatantly obvious actions and words. This is less of a problem for some; one aboriginal teen told me, "Prejudice is the other person's problem," but it can be a major source of anxiety for those who take the bigotry of others as a measure of their own self-worth. Parents need to be aware of the effects of such prejudice on their teens.

## The Need for Friends

Teens need friends in order to feel accepted, important, and real. As adults do, teens often need time to develop friendships, to find kinship with people their own age that they can trust and confide in.

Parents need to assess their teens' friends, but at the same time remember not to judge them unfairly, particularly on appearance. The shaggy, unshaven, ragged-clothed friend the teen brings home may have qualities he keeps hidden from adults but allows their friends to see. I managed to get past my own prejudices and the unkempt appearance of one of my son's friends and discovered he was a stock-market whiz who was interesting to talk to as well.

Many teens have a carefully constructed façade to effectively keep most adults from knowing them. Parents need to deal with their own prejudices. Admitting that they have some is a good first step to changing such preconceived ideas. Parents need to accept their teens' friends for who they are and what they may be willing to share. Parents must also not cling to their prejudices by justifying that because they are parents, they are right. It is not wise to insist that teens choose between family and friends; teens will inevitably choose their friends.

## The Social Group

When teens suffer from low self-esteem, they tend to gravitate to other teens who feel the same way. This is difficult for parents to accept or understand: what are they doing associating with those losers? But parents should understand that their teens have found a peer group and a place where they feel they belong.

Troubled teens have high dependency needs, so they need to have friends who include them in their lives. But if they think they are worthless and desperately want to be loved, some peers may feel threatened and withdraw, rejecting them. This drives troubled teens further into loneliness or into relationships with peers who themselves have such desperate emotional needs for acceptance that they accept bizarre behaviour in others.

The problem with relationships within these social groups is that the needs of individuals are so great that the members of the group are usually unable to help their friends until their own needs are met, thus, a teen may experience superficial acceptance, but basic indifference. In such situations, a teen's cry for help – "I'm going to kill myself" – may be met with cynicism – "Go for it, life sucks anyway" – instead of concern. But even with the inadequacies, a circle of friends is of vital importance to teens; without this group they are even more lonely, isolated, and withdrawn.

Sometimes teens will deliberately seek situations that reaffirm their low social standing, because they feel worthless and look for social situations that prove it. Teens with low self-esteem may also feel that anything they do, any social effort they make, is doomed to failure; therefore, they should seek what in their opinion is the lowest social situation they know of, since failure to assimilate into such a group will not be as traumatic as failure with a more desirable and admired group. They aren't risking much, so they won't lose much.

Parents should not cut off their teens' sources of friendship as a punishment. When teens are in trouble, they need their friends more than ever. If they didn't need those friends on some level, they would not be associating with them.


## How Parents Can Further Teen Friendships

As noted earlier, parents should not criticize their teens' friends. They, at least, are friends, and the teen needs them. Find something to like about them. Treat them as valued people. Be willing to learn from them. Parents should also make opportunities to get to know their teens' friends; they could include them on an outing such as swimming, skiing, or fishing. It is difficult for parents to include teens they don't approve of, but the experience will give parents a greater understanding of their own teens.

Parents should try to learn a new activity or skill along with their teens and their friends. In this way, parents allow themselves to appear vulnerable to their teens, making mistakes in front of them so their teens and their friends know that parents are not perfect. If the teens see that their parents can live with imperfection, they are more likely to accept imperfections in themselves, and realize that there is room in their lives for mistakes.

Teens may be tempted to join gangs that are focused around illegal activities and/or drugs. In such scenarios, parents should obviously not encourage such interactions, but they should also not overreact, which will reinforce their teens' attitude. Parents may need professional help in trying to extricate their teens from a gang.

Whether it's a gang or a more socially acceptable group, parents need to show respect and concern. If they are on a friendly basis with their teens' friends, they can, at a time when they are worried about their teens, ask their friends if they know of anything that would help. But parents need to establish a sense of trust and openness in order to make this happen.

### What is Independence?

Parents are expected to allow their teens to make independent decisions and at the same time stay involved with and be supportive of them. This is not such a contradiction as it seems.

It is an act of faith for parents to allow their teens to make their own decisions. They must let their teens fail, make mistakes, while at the same time showing them that they accept and support the teens. Parents need to look at the D in math their teen received and show that they understand that this is a problem, but not what the teen must do about it. Parents should listen, but not offer solutions.

If this seems too uninvolved, too vague, consider what happens if parents do become involved. If parents take responsibility for their teen's math mark and outline a course of studies the teen must follow, say from seven to nine o'clock every night, then the parents must oversee that it happens. This will affect the relationship between parents and teen in which the parents become the police. Thus, the teen isn't handling the problem, the parents are.

When parents simply listen, they have a much greater chance of helping their teens explore the causes of their problems, and from there, helping them solve them. Until the teens recognize their problems, they won't see the solution, and parents can't impose it.

Often, especially if communication has not been good, teens may tell their parents, "Nothing's wrong, I just got a lousy grade." It is enough for parents to express their concern that the teens are having trouble; if they don't want to tell you, they won't. Parents need to express the expectation that the teens will deal with the problem and that the parents have faith that the teens can.

## Religion as Control

Some parents use religion as a means of controlling their teens. They tell themselves they are only protecting their children from the dangers of the world as they impose rigid rules of conduct and try to push their ideas, ambitions, or morals onto them. Teens must accept these ideas in their own time, at their own rate, and in their own way. Parents can't use threats to get compliance with their rules and the rules of their religion without paying a huge price for it in the form of severed communication and withdrawal.

Parents can expose their teens to their religion and hope that the teens will use it to guide their own lives, but when parents utilize religious dogma to reinforce their authority, they run the very great risk that their teens will reject the religion along with the authority. Teens will know their parents are using religion as a means to control their lives.

Parents must ask themselves if they want their teens to develop spiritually, or if they want them to adopt religion so that the parents can be assured that the teens will respond to parental authority. If parents use religion to add authority to their own words, then they are in danger of forcing their teens to repudiate religion as they begin to attain an independent life.

If teens have the freedom of exploration, they may find peers and mentors within their religious community who will help them. A religious community is an excellent place for teens to find friends and adult counsellors. However, too much pressure to comply with rules and regulations will prevent this. Parents need to recognize that the teens' experience with that religious community is theirs alone, and they must allow them the opportunity to develop it.

## Parental Influence on Outside Agencies

Parents can ask at the beginning of the school term what kind of suicide education the school provides to its students. Parents can also leave books or brochures on suicide prevention around the house, or give them to their teens and their friends, and encourage school and public libraries to have displays of such materials.

Do teens know the people in their community who can help? Who are the counsellors at school, in the community, at the drop-in center? Do the teens know the crisis center number? Is there a youth line available? Teens need to know what groups are available to help them if they feel the need to talk, and can't talk to their parents about it.

Parents can also help the community by providing social services agencies (police, public health nurses, social workers) with the numbers of crisis intervention agencies and brochures and pamphlets on suicide prevention. All these activities should result in an increased awareness in teens of their responsibilities to each other when one of them is suicidal.

### PROFESSIONAL HELP

Parents of troubled teens may have assessed their family situation and decided that the family needs outside help. Like a car that isn't working properly, the family needs skilled attention. But unlike a car, the family cannot be driven to a counsellor and left for repair. It is not possible to transfer the entire responsibility for change to a professional, so parents should not expect it. Professional help needs to be accompanied by parents' co-operation and a willingness to accept criticism and new ideas.

### Commitment

In order to allow counsellors to help, parents must commit time and effort to understanding the problems and working them out. I recall one man who thought he was solving his family's problems by arranging an appointment with a psychiatrist for his wife and son and telling them to fix the situation. Since the problem centered around him, that plan was in trouble from the start. Usually both the parents and the teens are involved in counselling. Sometimes counsellors like to see members individually for some of the sessions, but, more often, the family goes together.

Parents need to be prepared for unexpected emotional disturbances, because many new issues are unearthed during counselling sessions. It is often discouraging to find that the first few sessions seem to cause more problems than were solved, unleashing more anger than anyone dreamed was hidden in the family. It seems at first that counselling makes the family situation worse, but it usually only clarifies it, showing the family what is already there. At this point some family members may want to quit. But it is important for everyone to understand the goals of the counselling and to be committed to those goals.

## Searching for Help

A friend of mine told me that her teenage son had been assessed at his high school as needing help. But she then spent six months going from school to doctor to agency, trying to find someone to see him. She was willing to pay, yet found "everyone in the assessment business and no one in the helping business." She thought people were more interested in impersonal tests than they were in the slow, methodical, yet useful process of listening and working through problems.

When searching for a good counsellor, parents are often too desperate for help to take the time to choose someone carefully.

One may be tempted to show up in the office of the first counsellor available without any idea if he or she will be helpful. It would be more useful to get references from a crisis center, a doctor, a family services center, or from friends, where possible.

### WHERE TO LOOK

In addition to the places listed below, other places to look for help include: the teens' school, the provincial or state registry for psychologists, libraries, women's and family centres, and the Internet.

### The Crisis Center
One of the best referral agencies is the local crisis center. A crisis center is readily available and can be reached quickly by telephone from almost anywhere. A crisis worker will have a list of publicly-funded family counsellors

and psychologists in the area or can help find such a list.

Almost all crisis center workers are good counsellors. They spend all day listening to people, and have training in how to do it well. They can offer a lot of help over the telephone, listening to problems, and offering ideas for solutions.

## Doctors

Parents often ask their doctors for help with their teens. Doctors should be good resources, available almost anywhere and easily found, but they usually don't have the time to counsel families, and very often are not skilled at it.

Several teens I interviewed had talked to their family doctors but did not find it useful. They received such comments as, "You're hurting your parents; smarten up," and, "How could you be so stupid." Negative responses like these dissuaded the teens from confiding in their doctors the next time they needed help. The teens' parents no doubt thought they were helping by sending them to the doctor.

Doctors may be more likely to refer patients to psychiatrists, MDs with specialized study, than to psychologists who are university trained in psychology but have no medical degree.

Psychiatrists are not necessarily better than psychologists, but they are very often covered by a medical plan when psychologists are not. Psychiatrists can prescribe drugs where necessary, psychologists cannot. Psychiatrists may not be able to spend as much time with a patient as psychologists can. As with all professionals, the degree of competence and ability to help depends on the individual one chooses more than on the profession they represent.

## Group counsellors

Some crisis centers have parent education groups, or they may participate in parent education groups run by other agencies. For some parents, a group situation is a reassuring reminder that other perfectly normal parents have similar problems. For others, a group situation can be an intimidating and embarrassing statement of failure, so such parents are reluctant to let anyone know how bad the situation is.

## School counsellors

The school counsellor is often a busy, overworked individual whose job description may include assisting students who want to drop, change, or add classes; giving in-service education to staff; arranging health films, guidance classes, and visiting lectures; and counselling students who have emotional problems.

While the job description does suggest that they are available to listen to students, the practical challenges of the job often leave little time for this. School counsellors rarely have medical or psychiatric support or regular conferences with psychiatrists or psychologists who can give advice on student problems. Their job is made even more difficult when parents are reluctant to discuss their teens' problems because they see a counsellor as a teacher in a school setting. When some parents enter a school building, even as old as they are, they are still reminded of the "them versus us" atmosphere of the classroom and may be reluctant to betray their children's weaknesses to the teacher, and to risk a written report in their records.

Most often, counsellors do not have time to effectively counsel parents anyway, and restrict the parent meeting to an effort to deal with behavioural problems, grades, or attitudes at school.

### Mental health counsellors

Mental health counsellors are available at family service clinics, state or provincial mental health centers, and private clinics. They may be nurses, social workers, psychologists, or trained workers under the supervision of nurses or psychologists. They are usually ready to provide long-term counselling and often have practical experience with adolescents. All counsellors are not the same; it may take time to find someone the entire family trusts.

Mental health clinics may offer group counselling or support meetings for teens and parents, or for parents only. A counsellor may be a member of the group and facilitate discussion and understanding. Groups are often set up to focus on a specific problem.

As with all helping groups and agencies, there are some that are not good. A friend of mine took her daughter to a city-run group in which all they did was play board games. On the other hand, another friend met with a psychologist who gave her a single suggestion that suddenly made her situation clear and acceptable. It is that kind of help that should keep families motivated to look for a good counsellor.

### Religious counsellors

Religious organizations may offer family or group counselling. Many religious services do not restrict their counselling to their own members, but are willing to help anyone in need. Counsellors may be ministers, priests, or rabbis who have some training in counselling, or professional psychologists or family counsellors hired by the church.

### Community health nurses

Community health nurses are available to anyone in most areas. Again, their talents and backgrounds differ. Some are excellent listeners while others are not. These nurses should be able to refer parents to appropriate counsellors and give them some idea of the availability and costs of different services.

### Social workers

Social workers may be good counsellors in some agencies, but generally state and provincial social workers are overworked and crisis-oriented. They respond to emergencies and are not able to take time with preventative measures. Like school counsellors, their job description may include applying for medical care, funding, housing and social assistance; handling daily telephone calls from schools, hospitals, doctor's offices, health units, and every other social organization in town; and filling out inter-office forms that justify the existence of the social agency to government funding bodies. This leaves little time for listening.

### Internet sources

There is a great deal of information available for parents on the Internet. The Internet is an excellent source for basic information which parents could use to help form their questions for a counsellor.

## Why Parents Don't Go to Counsellors

Parents may be reluctant to see a counsellor because they are unfamiliar with the counselling process; they have never visited one before and are unsure of how they should act, what they should say. Some parents believe that discussing intimate family matters with a stranger is inappropriate, may be reported to authorities, and is a betrayal of their family. They may be afraid that the counsellor will tell them to do things they can't.

Parents may feel that they will be forced into an awkward, unfamiliar situation that will rob them of dignity and any shred of control that they have been able to maintain over their teens. They see attending counselling sessions as a public admission of failure as a parent. One spouse may feel that a counsellor is a friend or ally of the other and that they will conspire to try to make him behave a certain way.

If parents have talked family problems over thoroughly before they seek counselling, the initial appointment will be much easier. Usually, though, parents use the counsellor to force the problem into the open because they are not able to deal with it, at first, by themselves.

Once parents find a counsellor who is helpful, the sessions should give them a tremendous sense of progress. Their teens should feel that their parents care enough to make great efforts to help, and the family should feel closer, more supportive, and generally stronger.

But families need to be aware that this process takes time. Having regular sessions with a counsellor implies that the family will move along a path of progress, but progress is usually accompanied by stress, conflict, and mixed reactions as family members struggle to make changes. The counsellor can hold a mirror up to the family so they can see their own dynamics in order to make those changes.

## RAISING A CHILD TO AVOID SUICIDE

### Feeling Accepted

We want to do all we can to keep our teens healthy, both physically and mentally. Just as we try to immunize them against disease, so would we like to immunize them against suicide. There is no guarantee that one's child will never try suicide, but there are some attitudes a family can adopt that create a climate in which suicide is a less likely option for teens. Teens should feel that:

- they live in a family atmosphere of acceptance;
- they believe their parents like them and are glad they are part of the family;
- someone is always willing to listen to them; and
- they feel confident and capable of dealing with the problems they encounter in their lives.

## Teaching Teens to Deal with Stress

One way to train teens to avoid the kind of turmoil that can lead to suicide is to teach them how to deal with stress. Because so much of what we teach is taught by example, parents must examine how *they* deal with stress. Do they react with rage? Do they internalize? If parents see stress as a normal part of life and project themselves as being capable of dealing with it, their teens will probably act the same way.

If parents have a hard day at the office, they should comment on it at the dinner table, then say how they dealt with it. But if a hard day at the office means they hit the bars in order to be able to cope the next day, then the parents are demonstrating that they have a problem dealing with stress, and are teaching their child to have a problem dealing with stress.

Because parents aren't perfect, it may be that the best they can do for their teens is to talk about their own difficulties with stress, and that there are healthy ways of dealing with it.

## Teaching Teens to Deal with Pain

In North America, we have a general aversion to pain, and go to great lengths to avoid it. If you have a headache, you must take an Aspirin; if you have a cut, you need a bandage. We teach our children that no one has to experience pain.

We take this notion further and tell them no one should have emotional pain, that happiness is the norm, and that unhappiness should be "fixed." Teens should be happy and pain-free at all times. Anything less is not normal.

Parents have supported this attitude by being quick to apply the bandage and to administer the headache remedy. In general, parents are more anxious to make the hurt go away than to support the child's method of dealing with it.

When, as a school nurse, I gave immunization shots, I explained to nervous kindergarten children, "Yes, it will hurt a little as the medication goes in, but if you take a deep breath and let it out slowly when I tell you, you can deal with it." They seldom panicked. These five-year-olds knew that an adult expected them to look after themselves, that she was sure they could, and they did. By actively handling their own fears and pain, they had more confidence to face the next fear, the next pain.

Dealing with pain is part of living. We know that, but we don't make it clear to our children. If we teach children to deal with pain by escaping in drugs ("Have an Aspirin"), by denying it ("This won't hurt a bit"), and by avoiding it ("Don't go to the party if you are embarrassed"), we do not equip them with the skills that they need as teens to deal with pain.

In elementary school, children gain confidence in their ability to handle problems by the small pains and disappointments they experience, and how they react to them. If parents teach their children to face their fears and anxieties, their children will learn how to cope when troubles arise. But if they haven't learned this, they will deal with problems in negative ways, such as escape, denial, or avoidance. As much as we try to protect children from frightening or painful situations, they do have to deal with them and need to be taught how.

Elementary school-age children trust their parents' advice. If you tell them that it helps to take a deep breath and count to five before they tackle a problem, they will try it. If you tell them to try to think of two choices as solutions to a problem, they will try it. Then they will feel that they are handling their own problems. Such small beginnings build great confidence.

Many children approach teen life with little experience in dealing with emotional pain. With laudable intentions of protecting their children, parents avoid situations in which their children may experience humiliation, anger, fear, or frustration. In some ways encouraging children to deny, avoid, or escape pain in the early years trains them to look for the ultimate escape in suicide. Teens often have the uncomfortable conviction that if they were really competent they would never feel pain. Confessing to feelings of hurt, anger, and humiliation is an admission of failure. If they are unable to express these feelings, they cannot get help in dealing with them. Many teens are so inexperienced in dealing with pain that they have a very limited vocabulary to describe it; they cannot even identify it, much less deal with it.

Teens need continual support and positive feedback when they handle a difficult problem, even if they don't do it perfectly. They need to know that their parents appreciate their efforts. It helps teens to realize that parents don't always handle all situations perfectly either. They need to hear their parents evaluating their own failures: "What I should have done was. . . ." "The next time I'll try. . . ." They need to see that everyone handles problems better on some days than others.

## Teaching Teens to Handle Loss

If children experience the loss of a relative, friend, or even a pet, parents need to explore that loss with them. Children need help in obtaining faith in their ability to deal with such loss. It is often a series of losses which are unresolved, unaccepted, or unexplored that culminate in a suicide attempt. Do not deny the importance of any loss. If teens will not talk about it, parents should at least let them know that they think it was important.

## Providing Networks

As children get older, it is important to build a program of activities and relationships that can act as a safety net when the child becomes a teen, and the burdens of decision-making become more explicit.

Young children are likely to be enthusiastic about almost any new activities, but teens are likely to be interested only in those activities they can do well. The more activities teens have that interest them, the more people they know, and thus the more competent they feel. Sometimes this is not true, however, there are teens who are very accomplished, busy, and active, but feel that nothing they do is ever good enough.

Parents need to consider whether the interests their young children pursue are their own choices so that their interest will continue into the teen years. Activities that were the child's choice, and for which the child had a great enthusiasm, will probably continue into high school.

## Pleasing Mom and Dad

Young children work for their parents' approval. If their parents' love and acceptance appears conditional on achievements, children will try very hard to achieve. But when they become teens, they may feel that the expectations of their parents, friends, and teachers are overwhelming, and will stop trying to please others altogether. Since they believe their acceptance and support from their parents was dependent upon achievements that are no longer relevant, the teens may suddenly find themselves without support.

## Increasing Self-Esteem and Confidence

The teen years are when parents need to demonstrate approval and affection. For many teens, the trouble they experience never equals the amount of love they receive from their parents. As children approach their teen years, parents should increase the amount of support they express at the same time they decrease the amount of authority they exert, so that teens feel that they are capable of handling most problems on their own while at the same time feeling supported by those who matter most, their parents.

It is not enough for parents to deal with their teens in the same way they dealt with them as children. Parents must reassess their actions, ideas, and relationships. It may be time for a new beginning.

Since teens say that their parents are very important to them, and that their relationship with their parents influences their decisions about life and death, parents need to look to the ways they interact with their teens and create a family environment that supports and helps them. Involvement with teens is one of the best strategies in suicide prevention.

# FIVE
## *The School's Role*

*She sits in the corner, her back to the wall*
*Students that whisper say nothing at all*
*She plays with her pencil, her fingers, her hair*
*The center of gossip in quiet despair*
*The teacher prejudges by where the girl sits*
*In the back by the window, she never quite fits*
*The teacher looks down with critical eyes*
*The girl smiles back, her face telling lies*
*The teacher tries hard to know the girl's thoughts*
*But never quite knows how far she is lost*
*Confused to the point where eternity ends*
*She doesn't need critics, she simply needs friends.*

– T.S.

When students look for help within their school communities they may run into the same kind of difficulties that Leslie did when her appeal for help to the school counsellor was ignored and the counsellor only spoke about her grades and her school absences. And Janet felt betrayed when the school counsellor discussed her problems with the rest of the staff.

Students need to be able to get help at school. It is essential that school administrators and staff recognize and acknowledge that suicide poses a very real threat to their students. This recognition cannot be taken for granted; there are still professionals in school systems who deny such a threat exists for "our students." Once administrators and staff accept the existence of this threat, they need to design and implement protocols for prevention, intervention, and postvention.

They must decide what formal classes on suicide prevention will be taught, what the attitudes of the staff should be, what appropriate responses to students might be, and how to make effective referrals. The extent of staff responsibility in this is crucial to implementing an effective program.

School staff need to know where they can go for help when they are worried about a student, as well as being able to recognize when a student is vulnerable. Not every teacher or staff member needs to counsel, but every teacher and staff member needs to use their skills to identify those students who need help.

The staff should know what emergency protocols to use and become familiar with the supporting professionals in the community. They also need to know what actions, attitudes, and conversations are recommended in the event someone in the school dies by suicide.

Every school should compile a manual of information on suicide prevention protocols, as well as provide in-service education time for staff every year. Many organizations have developed manuals and educational workshops so that schools do not necessarily have to create their own. Administrative staff should make contact with supporting professionals every year to make sure that the referral protocol works and that students will get the help they need.

## THE ROLE OF SCHOOLS

In the past twenty years many programs that address suicide prevention, intervention, and postvention have been designed to be offered in schools. Some programs offer education around the prevalence of suicide, its warning signs, and guidelines for dealing with students who are suicidal. As well, many schools have well-defined policies around procedure. This is a giant step from years past when school staff strongly believed that the best thing they could do was to pretend that teen suicide didn't exist and that by not talking about it it wouldn't happen. Now, staff realize that they have a responsibility to be involved. The prevalence of suicide in the student population suggests that we need to develop plans to help prevent it, as well as plans for dealing with those who are left after a suicide occurs.

Some programs, such as the Ronald Macdonald SOS High School Suicide Prevention Program,[1] are free. A survey of Internet sites can reference programs to study. A check with school district offices might reveal programs used in other schools in the district. The school librarian can research available programs. Mental health associations can recommend programs, and national suicidology organizations are worth researching as well.

## STAFF SKILLS

Workshops and seminars focused on teen suicide will help staff gain confidence as they get more information. Such programs allow staff to examine their own attitudes to suicide; some of us still have startling, judgmental attitudes, such as those who believe that suicidal persons are "selfish." As well, we have our own feelings of guilt, anger, and grief about suicide. In order to help students, staff need to explore their own feelings, attitudes, and prejudices, and deal with them. This needs to be done when staff are planning their crisis protocol, not when the crisis has occurred. It is true that a death by suicide in the school creates motivation for implementing an organized suicide prevention, intervention, and postvention plan, but obviously, such a plan would be too late for at least one student.

## WRITTEN POLICIES AND PROCEDURES

Once they have resolved their own difficulties around suicide – which is not an easy subject for any of us – school staff can be more effective in identifying youth who are at risk. They will be more likely to do this if they know what the school policies and procedures are for dealing with such students. Schools need to have written policies and procedures so that any staff member can easily see and understand the next step in his or her path to finding help. Schools should also be connected to a community of suicide experts, which may include educated volunteers and medical professionals. While I advocate a support team for staff, I do not recommend what Janet experienced, in which staff members discussed her problems with others in order to dissipate their own anxiety. Staff members need to know who the appropriate confidant is, and how this professional will help the student.

## THE SCHOOL COUNSELLOR

Very often administrators designate the responsibility for suicide prevention, intervention, and postvention to school counsellors, instead of spreading the responsibility throughout the staff where it properly belongs.

The teens I interviewed complained that counsellors were often too overworked or not educated enough in ways that would help them. Given that the number of counsellors per school is usually small, it is unlikely that they can be effective in dealing with a problem that involves so many students; all staff need to be educated and prepared to deal with it. Still, it is often the school counsellors who have the most urgent interest in information on suicide prevention, who have the appropriate background, and who spearhead preventative programs.

At the very least, counsellors should set up effective referral systems so that every student can reach a professional counsellor through a teacher, other staff, or a counsellor. Students might then be referred to a mental health worker, tribal counsellor, or school or community psychologist.

## COMMUNITY SUPPORT FOR SCHOOL PROGRAMS

Connections to the community are very important in this plan. Mental health counsellors can be of great support and guidance, and provide emergency help when students are in crisis. They are available at family service clinics, state or provincial mental health centers, health units, and sometimes private clinics.

While crisis centers are excellent sources of help for teens and their families, they can also provide assistance to school staff and students. Often, such centers have school-based programs that can help schools organize their suicide prevention, intervention, and postvention plans, as well as offer manuals and well-designed protocols for staff to follow. Training and support services are often arranged with school staff, and systems are set up so that schools can contact the crisis center in the event of emergencies.

## DOCTORS

Doctors can be a source of help for school staff, who may refer students in the event of trouble. But, as stated earlier, doctors are often not effective in helping students. It is important to be sure that referrals made by school staff result in help, not just an abrogation of responsibility. It is not feasible for teaching staff to assess the effectiveness of the doctor's efforts, but they should check in with the students to see if the referral was effective. If not, staff should perservere to find the student help elsewhere.

Much good work has been done over the last ten years in North America to increase awareness of the threat and signs of suicide among teens, but we are much less successful in advocating the responsibility of our schools and communities to offer help for students who need it.

## PEER COUNSELLING

An integral part of school suicide prevention-intervention-postvention programs may be peer counsellors – students who have had training in counselling, understand how to refer students for help, and are their confidants. Because suicidal teens are often more likely to approach a peer than an adult, such counsellors can alert adults to any potential danger as well as create opportunities for the teen to find professional help. Such peer counsellors need to be well-educated on the parameters of their responsibilities, have resources they can access, and know trusted adults to consult. They are not professional counsellors, but they may be the first person a suicidal teen consults, and thus can be life-savers.

## SCHOOL PROGRAMS

### Prevention and Intervention

For the most part, plans are detailed when they set out the protocol for intervention and postvention. Prevention is often assigned to formal classes and "taught" with videos and discussions a particular points in the curriculum. While this is useful, we need to view prevention as an ongoing process that moves very quickly into intervention, and be creative about the ways in which schools can help students. For many students

– visible minorities, gays and lesbians, and others – suicide is a result of continual persecution or bullying.

Bullying has received increased attention in recent years, and the connection between bullying and suicide has been reported in the media following the deaths of several victims of bullying who died by suicide. There are programs dealing with conflict resolution and bullying in many schools. What teens seem to need are islands of safety within the schools where they can find refuge from cruel and even dangerous persecution. These havens should at least be the classrooms, but as one student reported, "The teacher didn't want to see it. She'd turn away when one of the guys threw my stuff on the floor. Like, talk about giving permission!" Some teachers may be afraid or unwilling to confront bullies, or don't see it as part of their job. As a result, classrooms are not safe for many students. Staff needs to address this issue when they review their suicide prevention protocols. It is not enough to lead a class discussion after someone dies by suicide; it is vital to create and maintain a safe environment for all students.

Some suicidologists, such as White and Jodoin, advocate the cultivation of a sense of belonging to the school so that students see themselves as part of a "stable, supportive, orderly and understandable" community.[2] To achieve this sense of belonging, they advocate a program for incoming students that introduces them to the school and creates a nurturing relationship between the students and their home-room teacher. Teachers attend workshops before the school year begins to help them develop skills around counselling, emotional support, and team-building.

Such a program can help students see themselves as belonging to a positive social environment, as well as educating them on where to go for help when they need it. The success of the program can be measured in school attendance and student satisfaction as well as lower suicide rates for those who participate.

While many of the teens I talked to said that their parents did not care about them, and would not have responded to a teacher's concern, it is still necessary for teachers to try to enlist the aid of the parents. Teens aren't always right about what their parents feel or are concerned about. And even if they are right, the teacher still has an obligation to try.


## Postvention

Immediately after a students dies by suicide, school staff needs to put in place an already agreed-upon plan that involves naming one staff member, usually the principal, as the spokesperson, contacting the family, and announcing to students that a student has died by suicide if that has been the official pronouncement (while not cloaking the act in euphemisms such as "accident"). The school crisis team should be able to call on designated community helpers to assist in the coping plan. The goal of the plan is to keep as much dignity and privacy for the deceased student and his or her family as possible; to help staff and students cope with the trauma of the event; and to prevent copycat or contagion suicides from occurring. It is important that while grieving their friend, students not glamourize his or her death. While it may be tempting for some teachers to avoid talking about the event, it is necessary for students to have some time for discussion. Students should be given a chance to talk about the death with teachers as the facilitator of the discussion, but they need to be steered away from creating a martyr or icon out of the person who has died. "Copycat" suicides are a danger if the suicidal act is seen as noble, sacrificing, or dramatic. It is difficult for teachers to contain this notion because students want to put what they view as a rational, positive spin on what has happened, but it is important to emphasize the futility of such an act.

Students often display a wide range of reactions to such events. As well, trauma such as this can create widely fluctuating responses in teens, so the teacher needs to be prepared for what seems to be inappropriate or unexpected reactions, such as giggling or expressions of rage.

Teachers also need to be careful not to use the class discussion to vent their own feelings, but to allow the students to find their own language to describe their own feelings and to express their ideas. The language staff and students use to discuss suicide is important. For example, staff should be trained to avoid labelling suicide as "successful." Teachers also need to discourage the idea of memorials, mass attendance at the funeral, and other expressions of grief that can result in an over-dramatization of the death. Close friends should attend the funeral with their parents in their family group, but full class attendance is not wise. The school should not create a memorial for the student. These are more appropriate instigated and carried out by the family away from the school.

When teachers and other staff talk to students, they need to recommend counsellors, and steer students toward healthy coping strategies. Staff should follow a written protocol that they have learned on suicide prevention, intervention, and postvention. At the time of crisis, it is too late to discover the best way of coping; protocol needs to be in place before the event.

141

We should view school suicide prevention, intervention, and post-vention programs from the point of view of the students who need them. We have to know what it is like for students to go through the process of accessing help from school staff. Then we need to test out this process by imagining different scenarios to ensure the plan serves students.

School staff may feel overwhelmed by the needs of teens that appear to be psychiatric or medical concerns and thus beyond their abilities. While some teens may suffer from depression, bi-polar conditions, or schizophrenia, others who exhibit signs of trouble do not have mental illness. Compassionate teachers, even if they have no formal psychology education, can help students avoid suicide. If teachers become educated about suicide, and if their school has a well-defined plan with connections to community professionals, they may find that they can incorporate suicide prevention and intervention strategies into their normal teaching activities. While it may be onerous at times, it may also offer the gratification and reward of helping students which is, after all, their motivation for teaching.

# SIX

# Suicide Risk Factors, Attempts, and Completion

*I would hold your hand in the stormy skies*
*I would cradle your head in a hurricane of madness*
*I would wipe your brow and face the fire*
*and I would not relent, I would not relent ...*

*– B.B.*

## SIGNS AND SYMPTOMS

How close do teens actually get to attempting suicide if they admit to thinking about it? This takes an individual assessment. So many teens experience the feelings of hopelessness and isolation and try to cope in the same way that their behaviours can be warning signs to others that help is needed. We know that some situations or conditions make suicide more likely. For example, suicide is more likely around a teen's birth date; teens try suicide most often in the two weeks following their birthdays. One study reported that the likelihood of suicide in this period was three times more than expected.

None of the symptoms of suicidal behaviour that follow are necessarily indicators of suicide by themselves, but if symptoms are compounded in a person, the greater the possibility that person may be considering suicide – theoretically. It doesn't take into consideration how very different everyone is. There are some people who exhibit many of the following symptoms and never consider suicide – but enough do to make the symptoms at least an indication that suicide is a possibility.

We can think of these symptoms in the way we think of cold symptoms. People who have colds are not abnormal; their bodies are simply overwhelmed by the cold virus and they can't cope with it, so they show the symptoms of a cold. In the same way, a person can be invaded by numerous emotional problems which manifest themselves in suicide stress symptoms.

## Planning for Suicide

While teens differ from one another in personality and family composition, life experiences and goals, they often have similar reactions to stress and reveal similar signs and symptoms of impending suicide.

Teens may think about the possibility of suicide in general terms without seriously considering it for themselves. Those who are theoretically interested in suicide may talk about it without seeing it as an answer to their problems. Those who do see it as an answer give indications they are considering it.

Teens who have lost a family member to suicide are predisposed to think of suicide as a choice that is acceptable to their family, or to think that suicide is their destiny. Whatever the circumstances, teens who may be considering suicide demonstrate the following symptoms:

- They isolate themselves from others. They may watch television continually, listen to music for hours, or appear to be daydreaming all the time. They may refuse to talk, or develop monosyllabic speech patterns: "Yes," "No," "I don't know." Sometimes they ridicule others, or make sarcastic and vicious comments.
- They become preoccupied with death. They joke about it, write about it. They talk about death in relation to others, to wars or broad philosophical concepts. They may write poetry that contains allegories about death or English assignments that discuss it. They may buy music and play video games that are concerned with death, or wear T-shirts that advertise their preoccupation. While this preoccupation may have been apparent in the past, evidence of it increases.
- They have an increased number of physical ailments or accidents. These may be unconscious bids for help that are more socially acceptable than a suicide attempt. Parents, school staff, friends, and medical professionals often miss the teens' underlying despair and pay attention only to the broken arm or the painful ulcer.

- Changes such as addictions – increased drug and/or
  alcohol use; extremes of behaviour – suddenly more
  withdrawn or more outgoing; or moods – such as increased aggressiveness or passiveness. There may also be
  changes in friendships or involvement with peers; in
  sleep and eating patterns; in personal hygiene; in school
  attendance and performance.
- They may start displaying an emotional "deadness."
  They manage to exist in the family and at school without being touched emotionally by anyone, or reacting
  with any kind of passion or enthusiasm.

Parents, professionals, and friends often respond to the above signs
and symptoms in teens with frustration and anger. They may think the
teens are self-indulgent and weak, and they have difficulty understanding
behaviour like this as symptomatic of suicide, believing that "It's a stage,"
or "She's always like this," thus discounting the importance of such symptoms. But such symptoms need to be taken seriously.

### Suicide is Imminent

Teens who have tried suicide in the past are still at risk. Although it would
seem reasonable for parents to be alert to repeated attempts, some wrongly
think that people who have tried suicide and survived will not try it again
with the intention of dying. Whether they have tried before or not, here
are some danger signs that suicide is imminent:

- Giving away possessions. Teens will give away small,
  sentimentally-valued items as well as stereos, computers,
  and clothes.
- Making remarks suggestive of suicide. Teens will use
  phrases such as "ending it all," "getting out," "not being
  around to bother anyone." Remarks like these are difficult for others to interpret, since teens frequently use
  exaggerated language such as, "I thought I'd die!" on
  a regular basis. Parents and others may get used to the
  teens' overly dramatic language and may miss the real
  despair behind their words.
- Outright talking about suicide. Teens may talk to close

friends or family about their desire to die. They may leave written messages where family members or friends can find them, or talk to strangers in Internet chat rooms. Some even give details of their plans or leave messages to their friends there.

## The Trigger Event

Increasing stress can precipitate a suicide; that stress often comes in the form of some kind of loss. Often this loss is in addition to others that have occurred before. Regardless, the loss that exacerbates the teen's stress is known as the trigger event. It could be as trivial as losing an election at school or a canceled band trip, or as shattering as the end of a romantic relationship, or the loss of a parent in separation or divorce. It could be leaving school or moving to another one, the death of a loved family member or pet, loss of status, such as getting lower grades than expected or not making a team, or it could be the anticipation of trouble, such as a forthcoming court appearance or punishment for breaking the rules. Other triggers might be sexual abuse, a diagnosis of illness, or an accident.

Some suicide attempts occur at the diagnostic stage of a physical illness. Teens fear the loss of physical competence or beauty as a side effect of the illness or surgery. It only has to be important to the teen to be significant; it doesn't have to be understood as loss by anyone else. One girl I talked to was precipitated into a suicide attempt by her graduation from high school. She saw her friend, the high school counsellor, as being lost to her, and it was more than she could deal with at the time.

In their troubled state, teens are often unable to see at the time that life will get better. All that matters is the immediate, the here-and-now; they are convinced that there is nothing worth living for. They are not necessarily suffering from depression, but depression, a deep and overpowering sense of sadness and helplessness, can precipitate a resolve to die by suicide. It is useful to remember, though, that teens may contemplate suicide without experiencing major depression.

The relationship that exists between parents and teens at the time of the loss is of great importance to the teens' ability to deal with that loss. The less support teens get from their parents, the less likely they will be able to handle loss. One study reported that one-third of suicide attempts occurred after an argument with parents. Teens see the loss of parental support as vital.

Everyone has to cope with losses in their lives, but teens may not have the skills to know how. It may seem insurmountable to them, a crushing mountain of pain, as if their whole lives have become meaningless and rendered them helpless.

Teens need to stay connected emotionally to friends and family in order to deal with the often overwhelming despair they feel. It is not always obvious that they are experiencing this despair, so it is important for family and friends to keep continuous, open communication with teens, and to listen to them.

### Underlying Personal Characteristics

Many teens responded to their increasingly difficult lives by skipping classes and getting lower grades at school. Why go when you'll just get hassled for not doing the work? Others may make their personal appearance reflect their feelings of despair, such as wearing all black clothing, using heavy makeup, or having hair that hides their eyes. They may be trying on costumes to get out of their own skin, or using clothes as a screen to protect them from the world.

When teens feel they can't cope, they spend a lot of time daydreaming. Daydreaming can be a harmless escape for all of us, but it can also be symptomatic of a fantasy world that takes them away from real life. Many teens I interviewed remembered that just before they tried suicide they spent long hours daydreaming. They couldn't concentrate or pay attention to anything; they felt as if they were always half-asleep. Sometimes they had an out-of-body experience as if they were sitting back and looking at themselves going through the day.

Teens sometimes change their eating habits. They may stuff themselves, using food as a remedy for their problems, or starve themselves in the hope that they might disappear. Changes in sleeping patterns are also common, such as teens who have trouble going to sleep at night or find themselves waking early in the morning.

When the teens I spoke to were feeling rejected and depressed, they were prone to accidents. This might have been their way of flirting with death. Some of them started physical fights and had sudden bursts of violence; sometimes they attacked themselves, carving their arms with a knife, or cutting off the circulation to parts of their bodies. Sometimes their rejection of themselves was less obvious. They were very uncomfortable with compliments, for instance, and believed anyone who complimented them was obviously lying. They did things that invited criticism, like not doing like their homework, for instance, and then felt that the resulting criticism was because they were unlovable.

One of the problems of teens who have been rejected by their parents and who have low self-esteem is their firm belief that they don't deserve happiness. If they are happy, they are sure that it won't last; that is a sign of something awful on the horizon. Often they refuse to accept happiness and actively try to get rid of it.

Many of the teens had tried suicide more than once. As Suzanne said, "Once you try it, it's easier to do it the second time." Sometimes they tried something that didn't kill them immediately, but would at some time, like habitual drinking. Others engaged in dangerous activities that may or may not kill them, such as reckless driving, mixing drugs and alcohol, ignoring traffic, or walking on the outside ledges of buildings or bridges. They tried to hold death close with one hand while gripping hard to life with the other.

## Deaths of Relatives

As noted earlier, teens who are contemplating suicide may have, in the past, experienced death in the family – someone they cared about whose death made the idea seem comfortable. They may feel that by committing suicide, they will join that loved one in death. They have no assurance that this is so, but because they desire care and comfort so badly, they *believe* that the loved person will be waiting. They think they will have the "happily ever after" ending that they so desperately crave.

Some teens may have had a death in their family when they were young and were impressed with the way their parents reacted to that death. Maybe their parents showed no emotion at all except relief. Maybe they cried and proclaimed their love when it was too late. As young, impressionable children, some teens see such reactions and remember them. They may imagine that their parents would react to their death in the same way. Rarely do these teens have a chance to talk to anyone about how they felt at the time of the first death. They may be more likely to think that suicide is appropriate for them, or even their destiny.

Teens suffering from despair are often unable to describe what they are feeling. They often don't know if they are bored, angry, hurt, confused, or depressed, and may feel foolish revealing such thoughts to others. If the teens' usual method of dealing with problems is to get angry and say nothing or blame themselves, then they may see suicide as only what they deserve; that if they died, no one would miss them. Used to blaming themselves and looking no further than themselves for the source of their problems, they think that they aren't good enough to live. Their attitude is that they are worthless, and don't matter.

When parents, teachers, or other teens put them down, many take such criticisms seriously, since those smarter, more together people know the *real* person they are; if someone thinks they are worthless, then they *must* be worthless. It's as though they hold a mirror up to the people who matter in their lives so that they could see themselves, and that mirror reflected an ugly image which they believe is their true selves.

The self-esteem of the teens I interviewed was so low that every-day problems became proof that they were no good. They could not put themselves up against a thousand teens their age and tell themselves that they were really *all right*. They didn't *feel* all right; they felt second class. If anyone told them how good they were, they thought that person had poor taste and lousy judgment.

Self-esteem – feeling good about yourself, feeling valuable – isn't an absolute characteristic; everyone has degrees of self-esteem. It's common to say a person has "no" self-esteem, but "low" self-esteem is more accurate. People with low self-esteem expect very little happiness, while those with high self-esteem expect a lot of it. It seems that these expectations, or lack thereof, are to some extent self-fulfilling prophecies. People often set out to *make* happen what they *expect* to happen.

## WHAT OTHERS CAN DO

- Evaluate the risk of suicide. Talk to a concerned friend, counsellor, or other professional. It helps if the person who first recognized the problem discusses what they have observed with someone they trust and who knows the teen well, so that those close to the teen clearly un-derstand the risk.

149

- Ask if the teen is considering suicide. It is often hard to ask teens if they are considering suicide, but it is necessary. Talk about it. Let them "sound off," reveal their feelings. Those who talk about suicide to a compassionate listener are far less likely to attempt it than those who have no one to talk to. Most teens are relieved to be able talk about suicide. It may take them several attempts to reach out before they trust anyone enough, but they usually want to talk, and feel emotionally relieved when they do. Such conversations require those close to the teen to put their own reactions – such as hurt, anger, withdrawal, or denial – on hold in order to listen.

- Don't allow any opportunity for suicide. If parents think that suicide is impending, they must not leave the teens alone. Don't allow the opportunity or means to kill themselves available. The availability of the means for suicide – the gun, the rope, or poisons – greatly contributes to the possibility of suicide.

- Get help. As noted earlier, counselling for teens and their family can help. It is, at the very least, evidence for the teens that someone cares enough to try to get help. While counsellors are not always effective, those who are make a tremendous difference to the teen and their family. Parents need to be involved too, to get help with their own emotional needs at this time. They could find a friend to talk to so that they have some relief from the anxieties that the family situation is causing, or call a crisis center for advice and encouragement. They need to continue to assess the teens and the family situation for months.

A suicidal crisis is no time to allow teens to make their own choices if that choice is death. If they are having suicidal thoughts, teens are not able to make positive, rational choices. They need to have protection until they are able to function normally again. At some time, parents will have to "let go" and allow them the room to grow and make their own decisions, but it is not appropriate during a time of deep despair and cloudy perspectives.

- Stay involved. Parents or other concerned individuals need to stay close to suicidal teens, both physically and emotionally, in the months following a suicide attempt. Suicide takes energy, planning, and organization. Often teens wait some time after the first crisis, when they are feeling more energetic, before trying again. Parents and others need to continue to listen and to be available to the teens for a long time, even if the crisis appears to be over.

## BLAMING THE TEEN

It is tempting to blame the problems that led to a suicide attempt on the teens themselves: "She always had trouble"; "She never seems to cope." But teens are not islands; they are a product of the family's interactions. The teen's problems are the entire family's problems, and the family must find healthy solutions to them.

It is alarmingly common for those close to the teens to discount any first suicide attempt as an aberration that won't be repeated. They often underrate the teens' despair and deal with the suicide attempt by denying its impact. They may withdraw from involvement with their teens. The rationale for this detached attitude is encompassed in statements such as: "She's old enough to look after herself," or "She was only looking for attention." The conviction that the teens were "only looking for attention" seems to be an effective way of denying the situation's seriousness. By trying to categorize the suicide attempt as not serious, they excuse themselves from having to do anything to help. There is also an implication that if others paid any attention to the suicide attempt, they would only make the situation worse. Therefore, their inattention and lack of help is cloaked in the motivation of "concern." Their reason for adopting this attitude may be to protect themselves from having to face the problem. Such an attitude on the part of the those close to the teens exacerbates their isolation and despair and increases the possibility of second suicide attempt.

What should parents and friends do if they feel an attempt at suicide is imminent? There are some emergency measures that they should put into place.

## IN AN EMERGENCY SITUATION

### Before an Attempt

The first concern must be the teens' safety. Parents or those close to the teens need to protect them from harm. That may mean taking them to the hospital for advice on the severity of their suicidal symptoms.

Parents and others should also follow their own intuitive knowledge combined with their logical assessment of how serious the teens' problems are. If those who care about the teens feel they are desperate, they are probably right. At this time, if the teens insist, to the point of yelling and screaming, that they want to be left alone, parents and others should refuse. The teens are out of control; and those around them may need to assert more authority than they might want to.

If parents take their teens to the hospital to safeguard them but find that the situation is not as desperate as they have assessed, parents should not regret their decision to seek help. They may feel embarrassed by having "over-reacted," but this is far less a problem than feeling remorse for lack of action. The teens will have also learned that their parents cared enough to try to prevent their suicide. If the parents don't take action, the teens will be sure to feel their parents don't care.

Taking action may mean removing all potentially lethal objects from the house: medications, ropes, guns, razors, poisons, household cleaners, and alcohol. Alcohol in combination with other drugs can be lethal. Assume teens know all the possible hiding places in the house, and take all potentially dangerous materials away.

In an emergency situation, parents should not say, "I won't let you commit suicide; it's a silly thing to do," or other statements that are judgmental, belittling, or moralizing. Teens already may feel they are a burden, a nuisance, in the way parents should not give them rational arguments why they should not commit suicide; they will have more and better arguments why they should. Parents should tell their teens that they won't let them commit suicide because they are worthwhile and that they care about them.

If concerned parents or friends think the teens are so unsafe that even their presence won't prevent suicide, take them to the emergency ward of the hospital. If there is a choice of hospitals, they should call the crisis center and ask which one to use; some hospitals handle suicidal teens more effectively than others. Once at the hospital, stay with them; everyone needs an advocate in the hospital system to ensure that they get good care. And many nurses and doctors do not understand the problems of suicidal teens, and some can be judgmental, critical, and thoughtless in their comments.

The medical profession receives relatively little education about suicidal patients. Many seem to embrace the attitude that suicides are "a waste of medical time." Nurses and doctors sometimes feel that if they make the teens' treatment uncomfortable enough, even painful enough, the teens won't come back. This can strengthen the teens' resolve to avoid the hospital in the future, thus eliminating a resource that might help them.

Parents and others concerned should stay with the teens until a satisfactory plan that will keep them safe for the immediate future has been worked out with the hospital staff. No one should assume that suicide never occurs in hospitals, that the teens will be properly supervised, and will always have someone to talk to. They may be left unsupervised long enough to attempt suicide again.

### After an Attempt

If concerned parents or friends discover the teens after they have attempted suicide – after they have swallowed pills, or tried to hang or shoot themselves – emergency care is essential.

If pills were involved, call the Poison Control Center (the telephone number is on the inside of the telephone book) and tell them what the pills were and how many were ingested. You may need to induce vomiting; the sooner the pills are out, the better. Once at the hospital, stay with them until they are safe from immediate harm.

When their lives are no longer in immediate jeopardy, families should consider counselling. Resist the temptation to dismiss this suicide episode as a "one-time phenomenon," or the temptation to see the episode in isolation from the family. This suicide attempt may be a result of the family's dysfunction, not something that has occurred without cause. The percentage of those who repeat suicide attempts is high enough to motivate parents to change their family's patterns.

## WHEN A TEEN DIES BY SUICIDE

A teen who dies by suicide is a dreadful, tragic event which generates immediate compassion for the teen's family. At the same time, society often puts the blame on the parents themselves, as if the parents should have somehow prevented the teen's death. Parents are often convinced of this themselves. Siblings also may feel that they could have somehow stopped their brother or sister. It is often true that parents may have been able to stop a suicidal teen, so the tremendous guilt parents and siblings feel over the teen's death is very real.

Parents and siblings of teens who have committed suicide have trouble forgiving themselves for not being perfect. Sometimes they are judgmental, critical, indifferent, and abusive, but just as often they are not; they are no more incompetent as parents than most of us. I was surprised during my interviews of teens to find that many of their parents did and said the things most parents would think were appropriate, but that teens thought were devastating. It isn't possible to be perfect.

After a teen's suicide, their families must deal with an overwhelming sense of remorse. They need counselling and care, not only to deal with the death, but also to work out their own issues.

Again the crisis center is one place to get a referral. Mental health centres also offer counselling, in addition to psychologists, psychiatrists, and social workers. The school the teen attended may have a postvention program, and family and friends may be able to get advice and help from that source.

Some cities offer "survivors' groups" where mutual help is offered by others in similar states of loss and remorse. Groups such as these can help families work through their problems. There is no comfort in saying that parents will adjust and be able to forget the pain of a child's suicide. They will never forget it, but they may in time be able to live with it. And they may be able to help rule out suicide as a choice for the surviving family members.

We worry about our children; we educate them, cram them with vitamins, give them warm socks and hot milk, teach them, caution them, and love them in a great effort to turn them into confident, outgoing, intelligent, sensible adults. When we see that they are unhappy and have low self-esteem, we are often worried and angry that what we have done isn't enough. Very often, our intentions are admirable, but our skills are weak. Most of us didn't consider suicide as an escape when we were young and don't understand why our children do, especially when it seems as though their lives are so much more interesting and fulfilling than ours were. In many cases, we practice the habit of denial – "I don't want my child to be suicidal, so she isn't" – ignoring the signs and symptoms they show, the evidence of suicide in the neighbourhood and at school, the statistics for their age group.

It is obvious that suicide is a threat to everyone's child, that children don't have to be "special," necessarily mentally ill, or have obvious trouble to be vulnerable to suicide. When teens are suicidal, the signs and symptoms require immediate attention. Parents, teachers, and friends often need new skills to deal with the situation. Communities have agencies and programs designed to assist parents and friends in helping troubled teens.

There is no magic cure, gesture, or incantation that will make suicide go away, but if we learn to truly listen to our teens, their chances of trying suicide will decrease dramatically. Learning to listen uncritically and nonjudgmentally while at the same time accepting, encouraging, and trying to understand them is the single most important thing we can do.

*She could have died when she overdosed*
*Luckily not me.*
*She thought she was pregnant a couple of times*
*Luckily not me.*
*She was into drugs and booze and sex and fights*
*Luckily not me.*

*Can she make it before she cracks*
*and has no place to go?*
*She was on the streets a number of times*
*No warmth, no food, no clothes.*

*She was deserted more than once*
*She can't be me, she can't be me.*

– Diana

# Summary

## PARENTS

When I started this project, I hadn't realized how important parents are in the lives of teens. They seem to have tremendous power to make teens feel either good or bad about themselves. I thought that teenage suicide was a social problem; teens told me it was also a family problem. Some of the teens I interviewed chose to try suicide because it seemed a socially acceptable way to get rid of their pain. They may have had problems with their social group — which certainly influenced them — but their pull towards suicide seemed to be directly related to rejection by their family, rather than rejection by their social group.

I learned that I was as capable of ignoring teens' feelings as some of their parents. I empathized with them, recognizing how their parents had made life difficult for them, but realized that I had said some of the things to my own children that their parents had said to them. At different times in my children's lives, I had some of the same attitudes that their parents did, had slipped into the same patterns. These teens made me rethink my relationships with my own children.

I expected to find that teens' suicidal feelings stemmed from the pressures of competition, maybe a shallow social environment, a lack of direction and goals — almost anything. I hadn't wanted to hear what they told me, that the most difficult thing for them was the attitude of their parents. Generally, if their parents accepted them, they could deal with life; if parents didn't accept them, they couldn't.

I learned from the teens I interviewed that low self-esteem, and feelings of worthlessness, are not permanent personality traits. Many moved out of the difficult downward spiral of diminishing self-worth to find confidence and appreciation of themselves as human beings. They told me that they learned, slowly, to like themselves.

The teens interviewed felt a pressure to be happy, to be an expression of their family's worth by seeming to appear content. They often saw happiness evaluated by their parents in terms of material wealth and social status. They saw that their parents expected them to achieve academically and in the work force with a "good" job or a "good" career, but they saw little room in the job market for them, little chance of success in their parents' plans for them. Still, it wasn't their perception of the job market that was overwhelming, it was their parents' expectations of "super success." They didn't feel they had enough time to find their own way. Parents and teachers alike told them that they had to hurry, to compete, to be in the top percentiles or they wouldn't get a job — and they knew they couldn't do it.

So very often, no one asked them what *they* wanted, or how soon they wanted it. No one asked how they were coping, or helped them deal with pressures. I asked Diana and Steven if anyone had ever sat down beside them and asked, "What's wrong?" They looked at each other, reflected on their lives, then said that they didn't think so. They were usually *told* what was wrong with them. They had no chance to work out their problems with an understanding adult.

Teens felt they were accepted only when they met their parents' expectations, that they were accepted for the things they did well, but not for who they were. Their parents often demanded that they earn their love, a seemingly unattainable request. What they needed was parents who loved them and accepted them because they valued them, not because the teens had earned it. If unearned love was not available, the teens believed they were not "good enough." They believed they were not the person their parents wanted and would never be. Such a dangerous family situation made suicide attractive. To break this pattern in their lives they needed to understand that the pattern existed. They needed to face it, and they needed to talk.

## SCHOOLS

School violence such as bullying singled out teens as being unacceptable to society and thus made suicide an attractive option. Similarly, gay and lesbian teens and other minorities treated as socially unacceptable also makes them vulnerable to suicide. Social injustice was insidious in many teen groups. Prejudicial behaviour towards some teens resulted in a lesser feeling of belonging and an increased need to escape from it all.

Violence at school has increased in recent years, contributing to teens' feelings of not belonging, and increasing their stress and despair at being unable to cope with their daily lives. Teens at school have less supervision in the past, as well as more independence, more mobility, and the means to remove themselves from supervision at school and at home. In some countries they also have increased access to firearms, giving them the means to commit suicide. School staff need to be very aware of the realities of such violence and have protocols and procedures in place so they can help all students. Students also need to help one another.

## SOCIETY

One of the most important aspects of suicide prevention for teens in the larger society is the recognition by government and health authorities that teen suicide is a legitimate problem. With such official recognition, health authorities can designate funding for research and treatment programs. Health authorities can also establish expectations of health professionals to incorporate suicide prevention in their treatment of teens and look for accountability strategies that show whether the suicide prevention strategies are being implemented. Over the past twenty years, society has come to understand that suicide is a health hazard for teens, but we have not yet set into motion programs that would hold health professionals accountable for working to prevent it.

As a society we seem to be handicapped by the notion that individualism is sacrosanct and the right of the individual to choose to take their own life must be protected. We are less inclined to see the moral imperative of caring for the injured, the desperate, and the needy as part of our greater community and social commitment. We are less inclined to see a reduced individualism as the price we pay for greater social responsibility.

Now that we as a society are aware that teen suicide is a significant problem, we need counselling programs, protocols in school, parent education classes, crisis intervention strategies, and routine health surveys that find and treat those who are suicidal. It isn't enough to consider suicide a private matter that does not involve the community. As long as we have that attitude we will not take responsibility. Community programs are necessary to help families and teens prevent suicide.

The teens I interviewed taught me that most of the time help, a life-line, a way out, doesn't just happen. Someone other than themselves – a friend, crisis center worker, psychologist – made an effort. Someone listened while they talked, while they poured out their frustrations, worries, nightmares. In talking, they were able to face their problems and slowly work their way through to a solution.

We need a society where such people are available to all teens.

Most of the teens I interviewed had changed from despairing suicidal teens to much more hopeful ones. Life did get better for them. If others, the ones who are gone, had not completed their suicides, life might have changed for them as well. They needed more time, more friends, more hope, a society that recognized them and offered them help.

Time after time, the teens showed me their caring, sensitivity, and social responsibility. They impressed me over and over with their strength, determination, and tremendous courage. I wish I could hold them in reserve for every teen who contemplates suicide, because they would show them how much caring is part of the world. Perhaps it will help readers to know that those teens exist – thirty of them, hoping, caring, and wishing courage and strength on those who need it. Perhaps these teens are the adults of the future who will change society so that teen suicide is no longer an option.

# Notes

## ONE

1 USA Suicide Summary: 1999 Official Final Data, *iusb.edu/~jmcintos/USA99Summary.htm*
2 Statistics Canada, suicides, and suicide rate, by age group. Retrieved: *statcan.ca/english*
3 1993 World Health Organization. Retrieved: *www5.who.int/mental_health*
4 *a1b2c3.com/suilodge*
5 In *Health*, March 8, 2002. Retrieved June 2002: *News.bbc.co.uk/hi/english/health/newsid_1860000/1860453.stm*
6 Suicide facts, suicide rates along gender lines. Retrieved: *a1b2c3.com/suilodge*
7 Health Statistics: New Zealand Health Information Service. Retrieved: *stats.govt.nz*
8 Royal Commission on Aboriginal Peoples (1994). Choosing Life: Special Report on Suicide Among Aboriginal People. Ottawa: Canadian Communications Groups.
9 Government of Massachusetts. High School Students and Sexual Orientation Results of the 1999 Youth Risk Behavior Survey.
10 Durkheim, E. *Suicide: A Study in Sociology.* New York: Free Press, 1897, 1951.
11 Georges Minois. *History of Voluntary Death in Western Culture.* Princeton: John Hopkins University Press, 1999.
12 Patterson, I. & Pegg, S. Nothing to do: the relationship between 'leisure boredom' and alcohol and drug addiction: is there a link to youth suicide in rural Australia. Youth Studies in Australia, 18(2), 21–2, 1999.
13 USA Bureau of Health and Human Services. Retrieved June 2002: *a1b2c3.com/suilodge*
14 Fuse, Toyomasa. *Suicide, Individual and Society.* Toronto: Canadian Scholars' Press, 1997. Also Battin, M. P. *Ethical Issues in Suicide.* Englewood Cliffs, NJ: Prentice Hall, 1995.
15 Crook, M. *Please Listen to Me.* North Vancouver: Self-Counsel Press, 1988, 1992.
16 Suicide Facts, Encarta Explanation. Retrieved: *a1b2c3.com/suilodge*
17 Retrieved: *suicide-parasuicide.rumos.com/en/articles/statistics/stat00004.htm*

## TWO

1 Larry Frolick. *Splitting Up: Divorce, Culture and the Search for a Real Life.* Toronto: Hounslow Press, 1998.
2 Henry Giroux in Epstein, J. S. *Youth Culture: Identity in a Postmodern World.* Malden, Mass: Blackwell, 1998.
3 Suicide Lodge. Retrieved June 2002: *a2b2c3.com/suilodge*

[4] Retrieved June 2002: *corsinet.com/trivia/2-triv.html*

[5] American Foundation for Suicide Prevention, American Association of Suicidology. Retrieved July 2002: *asc.upenn.edu/test/suicide/web/3.html*

[6] SIEC Alert, July 1999, #36

## THREE

[1] White, J., & Jodoin, N. *"Before-the-Fact" Interventions: A Manual of Best Practices in Youth Suicide Prevention.* Vancouver: Suicide Prevention Information and Resource Centre of British Columbia, 1998.

## FIVE

[1] SOS High School Suicide Prevention Program. Retrieved July 2002: *mentalhealthscreening.org/sos_highschool*

[2] White, J., & Jodoin, N. *"Before-the-fact" Interventions: A Manual of Best Practices in Youth Suicide Prevention.* Vancouver: Suicide Prevention Information and Resource Centre of British Columbia, 1998.

# Bibliography

Bagley, C. and R.Ramsay. "Problems and Priorities in Research on Suicidal Behaviours: An Overview with Canadian Implications." *Canadian Journal of Community Mental Health* 4.1 (Spring 1985): 15–49.

Battin, M. Pabst. *Ethical Issues in Suicide.* Englewood Cliffs, NJ: Prentice-Hall, 1995.

Baumeister, R.F. "Suicide As Escape From Self." *Psychological Review* 97.1 (1990): 90–113.

Beautrais, A.L. "Child and Young Adolescent Suicide in New Zealand." *Australia and New Zealand Journal of Psychiatry* 35.5 (2001): 647–653.

Bradley, J. and M.J. Rotheram-Borus. *Evaluation of Imminent Danger for Suicide: A Training Manual.* Tulsa, Oklahoma: University of Oklahoma, NRC Youth Services, Continuing Education and Public Service, 1990.

*The California Helper's Handbook for Suicide Intervention.* Sacramento: The California Department of Mental Health Office of Prevention.

Canetto, S.S. "Gender Roles: Suicide Attempts and Substance Abuse." *The Journal of Psychology* 125.6 (Nov 1991): 605–620.

Chandler, M. "Self-continuity In Suicidal and Non-Suicidal Adolescents." *New Directions for Child Development* 64 (Summer 1994): 55–69.

Chandler, M. and C. Lalonde. "Cultural continuity as a hedge against suicide in Canada's First Nations." *Transcultural Psychiatry* 35.2 (1998): 191–219.

Coleman, D. Lecture on Addictions. New Westminster, BC, 1997.

Cooper, M., A.M. Karlberg, and L. Pelletier Adams. *Aboriginal Suicide in British Columbia.* Burnaby, BC: BC Institute on Family Violence Society, 1991.

Curran, D. *Adolescent Suicidal Behavior.* Washington: Hemisphere Publishing Corporation, 1987.

Dunlop, R.L. *The Selfish Brain.* Center City, MN: Hazelden, 1997.

Eggert, L., E. Thompson, B. Randall, and K. Pike. "Preliminary Effects of Brief School-Based Prevention Approaches for Reducing Youth Suicide: Risk Behaviors, Depression, and Drug Involvement." *Journal of Child and Adolescent Psychiatrisc Nursing* 16.2 (2002): 43–64.

Epstein, J.S. *Youth culture: Identity in a Postmodern World.* Malden, MA: Blackwell, 1998.

Erikson, E. *Identity: Youth and Crisis.* New York: Norton, 1968.

Evans, W.P., R.M. Marte, S. Betts, and B. Silliman. "Adolescent Suicide Risk and Peer-Related Violent Behaviors and Victimization." *Journal of Interpersonal Violence* 16.12 (2001): 1330–1348.

Evoy, J.J. *The Rejected: Psychological Consequences of Parental Rejection.* University Park, PA: The Pennsylvania State University Press, 1981.

Frolick, L. *Splitting up: Divorce, Culture and the Search For a Real Life.* Toronto: Hounslow Press, 1998.

Fuse, T. *Suicide, Individual and Society.* Toronto: Canadian Scholars' Press, 1997.

Gould. M.S. and D. Shaffer. "The Impact of Suicide in Television Movies." *The New England Journal of Medicine* 315.11 (11 Sept 1986): 690–694.

Grover, H.J. and W.J. Berkan. *A Guide to Curriculum Planning in Suicide Prevention.* Madison, WI: Wisconsin Department of Public Instruction, 1990.

Grunbaum, J.A., L. Kann, S.A. Kinchen, B. Williams, J.G. Ross, R. Lowry, and L. Kolke. "Youth Risk Behavior Surveillance – United States, 2001." *MMWR: Morbidity and Mortality Weekly Report* 51.4 (2002): 1–62.

*Healing Journey.* Ottawa: Mental Health Advisory Services, Medical Services Branch, Health Canada, 1993.

Hendin, H. *Suicide in America.* New York: W.W. Norton, 1995.

Hulten, A., G. Jiang, D. Wasserman, K. Hawton, H. Hjelmeland, D. DeLeo, A. Ostamo, E. Salancer-Renbery, and A. Schmidtke. "Repetition of Attempted Suicide Among Teenagers in Europe: Frequency, Timing and Risk Factors." *European Child & Adolescent Psychiatry* 10.3 (2001): 161–169.

Kienhorst, I. "Kurt Cobain." *Crisis: The Journal of Crisis Intervention and Suicide Prevention* 15.2 (1994): 62–64.

Kirmayer, L. *Suicide Prevention and Mental Health Promotion in First Nations and Inuit communities.* Montreal: Culture & Mental Health Research Unit, Institute of Community & Family Psychiatry, Sir Mortimer B. Davis-Jewish General Hospital, 1999.

Konopka, G. "Adolescent Suicide." *Exceptional Children* 49.5 (Feb 1983): 390–94.

Kroger, J. *Identity in Adolescence: The Balance Between Self and Other.* New York: Routledge, 1996.

Krug, E. *World Report on Violence and Health.* Geneva: World Health Organization, 2002.

LaDue, R.A. "Coyote Returns: Twenty Sweats Does Not an Indian Expert Make." *Bringing Ethics Alive: Feminist Ethics in Psychotherapy Practice, Women and Therapy* 15.1 (1994): 93–111.

Leenaars, A. *Suicide in Canada.* Toronto: University of Toronto Press, 1998.

Lester, D. *Why People Kill Themselves: A 2000 Summary of Research on Suicide.* 4th ed. Springfield, IL: Charles C. Thomas, 2000.

Lester, D. *The Cruelest Death: The Enigma of Adolescent Suicide.* Philadelphia: Charles Press, 1992.

Madge, N. "Youth suicide in an international context." *European Child & Adolescent Psychiatry* 8.4 (1999): 283–291.

Masecar, D. *Northern Lifelines: Suicide Information and Resource Manual.* Sault Ste Marie, ON: Algoma Child and Youth Services, 1992.

Minois, G. A *History of Suicide: Voluntary Death in Western Culture.* Trans. Lydia Cochrane. Princeton: John Hopkins University Press, 1999.

Nohler, B. and F. Earls. "Trends in Adolescent Suicide: Misclassification Bias?" *American Journal of Public Health* 91.1 (2001): 150–153.

Patterson, I., and S. Pegg. "Nothing To Do: The Relationship Between 'Leisure Boredom' and Alcohol and Drug Addiction: Is There a Link to Youth Suicide in Rural Australia." *Youth Studies in Australia* 18.2 (1999): 21–2.

Pickering, W.S.F. *Durkheim's Suicide: A Century of Research and Debate.* New York: Routledge, 2000.

Pfeffer, C.R. *The Suicidal Child.* New York: The Guilford Press, 1986.

Ramsay, R. *Suicide Intervention Handbook.* Calgary, AB: LivingWorks Education, 1997.

Rew, L., M. Taylor-Seehafer, and M.L. Fitzgerald. "Sexual Abuse, Alcohol and Other Drugs Use, and Suicidal Behaviors in Homeless Adolescents." *Issues in Comprehensive Pediatric Nursing* 24.4 (2001): 225–240.

Rotherram-Borus, M.J., J. Bradley, and N. Obolensky. *Planning to Live: Evaluating and Treating Suicidal Teens in Community Settings.* Tulsa, OK: National Resource Center for Youth Services, University of Oklahoma, 1990.

Royal Commission on Aboriginal Peoples. *Choosing Life: Special Report on Suicide Among Aboriginal People.* Ottawa: Canadian Communications Groups, 1994.

Royal Commission on Aboriginal Peoples. *The Path to Healing: Report of the National Round Table on Aboriginal Healing and Social Issues.* Ottawa: Royal Commission on Aboriginal Peoples, 1993.

Russell, S.T. and K. Joyner. "Adolescent Sexual Orientation and Suicide Risk: Evidence From a National Study." *American Journal of Public Health* 91.8 (2001): 1276–1281.

Shneidman, E. *Comprehending Suicide: Landmarks in 20th-Century Suicidology.* Washington, DC: American Psychological Association, 2001.

Shamoo, T.K. and P. Patros. *I Want to Kill Myself: Helping Your Child Cope With Depression and Suicidal Thoughts.* Lexington, MA: Lexington Books, 1990.

Stack, S., J. Gundlach, and J.L. Reeves. "The Heavy Metal Subculture and Suicide." *Suicide and Life-threatening Behavior* 24.1 (Spring 1994): 15–23.

Stimming, M.T. *Before Their Time: Adult Children's Experiences of Parental Suicide.* Eds. Mary Stimming and Maureen Stimming. Philadelphia: Temple University Press, 1999.

*Strengthening the Circle: What Aboriginal Albertans Say About Their Health.* Edmonton: Aboriginal Health Unit, Alberta Health, 1995.

*Suicide in Canada: Report on the National Task Force on Suicide in Canada.* Ottawa: Mental Health Divisions, Health Services and Promotion Branch, Health and Welfare Canada, Minister of National Health and Welfare, 1987.

Thatcher, W.G., B.M. Reininger, and J.W. Drane. "Using Path Analysis to Examine Adolescent Suicide Attempts, Life Satisfaction and Health Risk Behavior." *Journal of School Health* 72.2 (2002): 71–77.

Trovato, F. A. *Durklheimian Analysis of Youth Suicide in Canada.* Edmonton, AB: Population Research Laboratory, 1992.

Tuk, T.A. *Suicide, Homicide, and Gun Deaths, British Columbia: 1985–1993.* Victoria, BC: Division of Vital Statistics, Ministry of Health and Ministry Responsible for Seniors, 1995.

van de Wetering, S. "Implicit Assumptions in Theories of Prejudice." Diss. Simon Fraser University, 1997: 1–116.

Violato, C. and L. Travis. *Advances in Adolescent Psychology.* Calgary, AB: Detselig Enterprises, 1995.

White, J. and D. Rouse. *Data Report On the Psychosocial Characteristics of Completed Suicides in British Columbia.* Vancouver: Suicide Prevention Program at CUPPL, UBC: 114, 1997.

White, J, and N. Jodoin. *"Before-the-Fact" Interventions: A Manual of Best Practices in Youth Suicide Prevention.* Vancouver: Suicide Prevention Information and Resource Centre of British Columbia, 1998.

White, T. *How to Identify Suicidal People: A Systematic Approach to Risk Assessment.* Philadelphia: Charles Press, 1999.

Williams, J.M. *Cry of Pain: Understanding Suicide and Self-Harm.* London: Penquin Books, 1997.

*Working Together Because We Care: Rankin Inlet Forum.* Yellowknife, NT: Northwest Territories Social Services, 1992.

*Youth Suicide Prevention Programs: A Resource Guide.* Atlanta: Public Health Service Centers for Disease Control, National Center for Injury Prevention and Control, 1992.

## INTERNET SOURCES

*Health Statistics.* New Zealand Health Information Service. <nxhis.govt.nz/stats/
youthsuicide.html>

*High School Students and Sexual Orientation Results of the 1999 Youth Risk Behavior Survey.* Government of Massachusetts. Jul 2002 <state.ma.us/gcgly/yrhsfl99.html>

*In Health.* 8 March 2002. June 2002 <News.bbc.co.uk/hi/english/health/newsid_1860000/
1860453.stm>

The National Strategy For Suicide Prevention. <mentalhealth.org>

*Suicide Facts, Encarta Explanation.* <a1b2c3.com/suilodge/facenc1.htm> also <suicid-
parasuicide.rumos.com/en/articles/statistics/stat00004.htm>

*Suicide Facts, Suicide Rates Along Gender Lines.* Aug 2002 <a1b2c3.com/suilodge/facgen1.htm>

Suicide Information and Education Centre, Calgary, AB. <siec.ca>

Suicide Lodge. June 2002 <a1b2c3.com/suilodge/figus1.htm>

*Suicides and Suicide Rate, By Age Group.* Statistics Canada. July 2002 <statcan.ca/english/Pgdb/
People?health/health01.htm>

*USA Suicide Summary: 1999 Official Final Data.* <iusb.edu/~jmcintos/USA99Summary.htm>

US Bureau of Health and Human Services. June 2002 <a1b2c3.com/suilodge/facgen1.htm>

*US Suicide Rates by Age, Gender and Racial Group.* Oct 2002 <nimh.nih.gov/research/suichart.cfm>

Watkins, Carol. *Suicide and the School.* Oct 2002 <baltimore.psych.com/Suicide.htm>

World Health Organization 1993. <www.who.int/mental_health/main.cfm>

Marion Crook has a PhD in Education from the University of British Columbia. She spent the last fifteen years actively researching the numerous difficulties and challenges teens face. *Out of Darkness* is her 23rd published book. Also available from Arsenal Pulp Press is *The Face in the Mirror: Teens and Adoption.* She teaches university in Surrey, BC while continuing to research and write.